Fantastic Ferraris

Fantastic Ferraris

Antoine Prunet
Peter Vann

Motorbooks International
Publishers & Wholesalers Inc.
Osceola, Wisconsin 54020, USA ®

Other books by Antoine Prunet:

Ferrari Sport Racing and Prototypes Competition Cars
The Ferrari Legend: The Road Cars

First published in English in 1988 by Motorbooks International Publishers & Wholesalers Inc, P O Box 2, 729 Prospect Avenue, Osceola, WI 54020 USA

First published in French in 1987 by Editions Presse Audiovisuel

Printed in Belgium
Bound in France

The information in this book is true and complete to the best of our knowledge. All recommendations are made without any guarantee on the part of the author or publisher, who also disclaim any liability incurred in connection with the use of this data or specific details

We recognize that some words, model names and designations, for example, mentioned herein are the property of Ferrari Esercizio Fabbriche Automobili e Corse SpA. We use them for identification purposes only. This is not an official publication

Library of Congress Cataloging-in-Publication Data
Prunet, Antoine.
  [Ferrari fantastiques. English]
  Fantastic Ferraris / Antoine Prunet, Peter Vann.
    p.   cm.
  Translation of: Ferrari fantastiques.
  ISBN 0-87938-327-5
  1. Ferrari automobile—Pictorial works.   2. Ferrari, s.p.a.-
-History. I. Vann, Peter. II. Title.
TL215.F47P7713 1988   88-21520
629.2'222—dc19   CIP

On the cover: Ferrari 410 Sport. *Peter Vann*

Motorbooks International books are also available at discounts in bulk quantity for industrial or sales-promotional use. For details write to Special Sales Manager at the Publisher's address

Contents

Preface

———

The prestige enjoyed by Ferrari today is phenomenal. In just forty years, the Italian marque has become synonymous with greatness in the automobile world. Yet the source of this fame is elusive; it is not due solely to the age of the company, its number of race victories, nor even to its avant-garde styling. In fact, many manufacturers have surpassed Ferrari on these points. The explanation for the Ferrari phenomenon lies elsewhere, in the permanency of vision of the man behind the cars.

Enzo Ferrari has always been devoted to motor racing. Cars bearing the Cavallino insignia have entered everything from Formula 1 and 2 Grand Prix to endurance races and hill climbs. This commitment has continued without interruption since 1947, winning both first-place laurels and also-ran finishes. No other manufacturer today can claim such a heritage, indispensible for prestige.

Are all Ferraris fantastic? I would not attempt to prove the contrary to the reader who has just opened this book; some are more fascinating than others, however. Not just because of their rarity—small circulation can mean the same as failure—but because of the mark they have left on their epoch and the influence they have had on other Ferraris, not to mention other makes of cars.

For some people, the most prestigious Ferraris are the Scuderia Ferrari cars, the cars exclusively used by the Maranello racing team. These "factory" Ferraris, which rarely numbered more than half a dozen per season, only left Maranello for testing and racing. They were automatically returned to the factory to be continually developed and, sometimes, repaired. In the end, they formed the base for the limited range of vehicles made for customers. These factory Ferraris—which were always testbeds in a permanent state of evolution—are naturally the most revolutionary as well. They are also often the most interesting, since they are, so to speak, original works; the derivatives, even if small in number, will only ever be reproductions. Finally, since they were driven by revered racing drivers, they are associated with the greatest victories.

Ferrari has also forged a prestigious name for itself in the world of private cars. Though derived from racing cars, production Ferraris are of a different nature. More public, or less scientific, they have brought the world of dreams back to driving and made a significant contribution to the firm's prestige. In the production cars, the constant search for the fantastic has been conducted not only in terms of technique but also of style. No one can deny the importance of the designer to the Ferrari image, the foremost being Pininfarina, which left its avant-garde stamp on so many vehicles. Unique and moving designs were translated first into prototypes, and then sometimes into limited production. By attracting an elite clientele, the production Ferraris pointed the way to the future.

These criteria have guided us in our choice of cars for this book. The Ferraris in the following pages—some little-known, some famous—seem to us to have been the most influential in creating the legend.

Antoine Prunet

Ferrari owners and Ferraris

Ferrari owners—from the pioneers to today's enthusiasts to the collectors—have all contributed to the prestige of the Italian make.

Twenty years ago, secondhand Ferraris were often regarded as nothing more than used cars. The most astute—but not necessarily the richest—purchasers have changed this state of affairs; what was once a secondhand car is now a collector item, even a work of art. Although it may not be up to us to congratulate them, we are keen on sincerely thanking these enthusiasts. They have saved these precious objects and resurrected their status. We also thank them for their assistance in the creation of this book.

We argued with French Ferrari connoisseur Pierre Bardinon. "Why this one rather than that one? Why not all of them?" he wanted to know. Bardinon wanted to be sure of our choices so he could make available the vehicles of the Mas du Clos collection from the Fondation Cartier. The fact that they are not all included in this book is due to a shortage of time and space.

Albert Obrist does not allow himself to collect and will not permit the word "museum" to be used. He has simply gathered his favorite Ferraris, not only for their beauty but also to drive them as they should be driven and to equal—and sometimes beat—the best times on the clock. From the circuits of Imola, Dijon and Mugello, where he drives regularly, to the glaciers of his native Oberland and the small airports of Switzerland, where speed is unrestricted (with authorization), he has set them free for us once more. Albert Obrist's six Ferraris, combined with Peter Hauberger's 500TRC and 512M, put Switzerland in second place in this book.

Pascal Motte is a new collector with ambition. His Ferraris have aided him in discovering the joys of driving. As soon as he could escape from his business, he rushed to Croix-en-Ternois. On his return that day, he was a bit surprised by the location chosen by Peter Vann to photograph his cars.

Three Ferraris from Paris are included. Antoine Midy and Christian Philippsen deserve credit for the exacting maintenance of their exclusive vehicles.

Antoine Raffaelli took two fabulous Ferraris out of the Musee de l'Automobiliste for us: Adrien Maeght's 860 Monza and Andre Binda's 512.

A New York friend had to persuade his assistant from Reno, Nevada, who was overwhelmed by the coming Pebble Beach Concours d'Elegance, to move eight vehicles so as to be able to bring out Peter Collins' "cafe racer."

When we asked Steve Tillack whether, by any chance, he had "Bertone number two," he replied, "I have both the Bertones at present. Whenever you like."

Three other Californians were also generous with their assistance and dressed up their Superamericas and Superfasts for photographic sessions: James Truitt, Donald Ernst and Greg Garrison.

The chain of American help continued eastward with Bob Bodin in Minneapolis, Wayne Golomb in Chicago, and Luigi Chinetti, father and son, in Connecticut.

Between two trips, Mark Tippetts became our voluntary ambassador in England. He organized photographing Dudley Mason-Styrron's Dino 206S and Clive Beecham's ex-Rob Walker 250GT for Peter Vann.

We must also mention Christian Garnier-Collot and Kodak who helped Peter Vann in his shots and Serge Belly for his inexhaustible documentation.

Colombo versus Lampredi: equality

Before reaching the 4.5 liters which would change Ferrari's destiny in Formula 1, the engine went through several intermediary stages. Engineer Aurelio Lampredi first limited himself to a capacity of 3322 cc with a 68 mm stroke and a 72 mm bore. Luigi Bazzi, the faithful and indispensable link between drawing board and racing track, installed this engine in two Touring-designed barchettas which were entered in the Mille Miglia on April 23, 1950, and driven by Alberto Ascari and Luigi Villoresi. Both cars dropped out due to transmission failure. An interim 3.3 liter engine reappeared two months later at the Belgian Grand Prix, this time in a single-seater piloted by Ascari. In the "old" 125C with its two-stage compressor, Villoresi could only finish sixth

The 375F1, a new future in Ferraris.

after Ascari. The Alfa Romeo Alfettas were still in front, but Ferrari's new direction was proven.

The capacity of the new engine was increased to 4080 cc by enlarging the bore to 80 mm; the power jumped from 280 to more than 320 horsepower. This engine was granted its first run, on the streets of Geneva on July 30 for the 1950 Grand Prix des Nations. During practice, Ascari with a 4.1 liter car and Villoresi with a 3.3 liter car placed the two Ferraris behind Juan Manuel Fangio's Alfetta and in front of three other Alfa Romeos. In the race, however, Villoresi destroyed the 3.3 liter engine and Ascari broke the new engine.

The final development stage came in September 1950. The twelve-cylinder engine was

Enzo Ferrari and one of the first 375F1s on the Modena "aerautodromo." Does the angle of Ferrari's hat indicate optimism?

given its definitive capacity—4493.7 cc—thanks to an increased stroke of 74.5 mm, while the 80 mm bore was unchanged. Fittingly, it was the fans at Monza who first saw the two new Ferraris at the 1950 Italian Grand Prix. Ascari was at the wheel of one car while Villoresi, who was unavailable following an accident in Geneva, was replaced in the other by Dorino Serafini, the Maranello test driver. Alfa Romeo had two new 159s (an updated version of the 158) driven by Fangio and Nino Farina. In practice, Ascari was evenly matched with Fangio, but the two leaders broke down while vying to dominate the race. Ascari took over Serafini's car, which was lagging behind, and finished second to Farina by a narrow margin.

The Ferrari that was finally able to threaten the reign of the Alfa Romeos was born in less than six months. It was called the 375F1 in accordance with its cylinder capacity, and its general form was basically defined. Surmounted by three Weber 40 DCF carburetors and with a compression ratio of 11:1, the long-stroke 4.5 liter car boasted 330 horsepower, which it transmitted to the rear wheels via a multiple-disc dry clutch and a four-speed gearbox coupled to a ZF self-locking differential. The chassis, with tubular side frames, front wishbone suspension, transverse leaf spring and Houdaille hydraulic shock absorbers, was classic Ferrari. On the other hand, the

A Ferrari to dethrone the Alfettas

de Dion rear axle guided by a slide firmly attached to the differential cage, was a 1950 innovation and was to remain a distinctive feature of single-seater Ferraris and other Sports racing cars.

The last Formula 1 race of the 1950 season took place at Barcelona and produced a Ferrari 375 double win, Ascari and Serafini in that order—but the Alfa Romeos did not race. Ferrari's goal was still to be achieved: to beat Alfa Romeo in the Formula 1 world championship, which had just been created, in the 1951 season.

Imola 1987. Like Silverstone 1951, an early test session.

Meanwhile, Ferrari engineer Giocchino Colombo had returned to Alfa Romeo and was working hard on the Alfettas. After some non-championship races at which the two protagonists traded off wins, but always in the absence of the other, Ferrari modified the fixed cylinder heads of the 4.5 liter engine. The new heads used twenty-four spark plugs instead of twelve, thereby gaining about thirty horsepower. The Alfa Romeo 159Ms (modified) won the first three grand prix, the Swiss Grand Prix at Berne, the Belgian Grand Prix at Spa and the European Grand Prix at Reims. But in the fourth round of the 1951 world championship, the English Grand Prix at Silverstone on July 14, Argentine Froilan Gonzales gave Ferrari its first victory. Ascari repeated the achievement two weeks later on the Nurburgring for the German Grand Prix and again on September 16 at Monza for the Italian Grand Prix.

According to all forecasts, the 4.5 liter Ferraris, with their dual ignition, were favorites for the last round, the Spanish Grand Prix. But on the Catalan circuit of Pedralbes, the four 375F1s, the one after the other, were slowed by tire trouble. The Ferraris could not make up lost time, even with the higher fuel consump-

Twelve cylinders and twenty-four spark plugs

tion of the supercharged Alfettas which forced the Alfas to refuel an extra time. Ascari finished fourth, with a total of only twenty-five points, compared with Fangio's thirty-one. Alfa Romeo had beaten Ferrari for the first world title.

Colombo had his revenge on Lampredi, but this confrontation between the two Italian makes was the first and the last. Alfa Romeo did not reappear in the two following championships, which were in Formula 2 and limited to two liters. Ascari would go it alone with the 500F2, a four-cylinder designed by Lampredi.

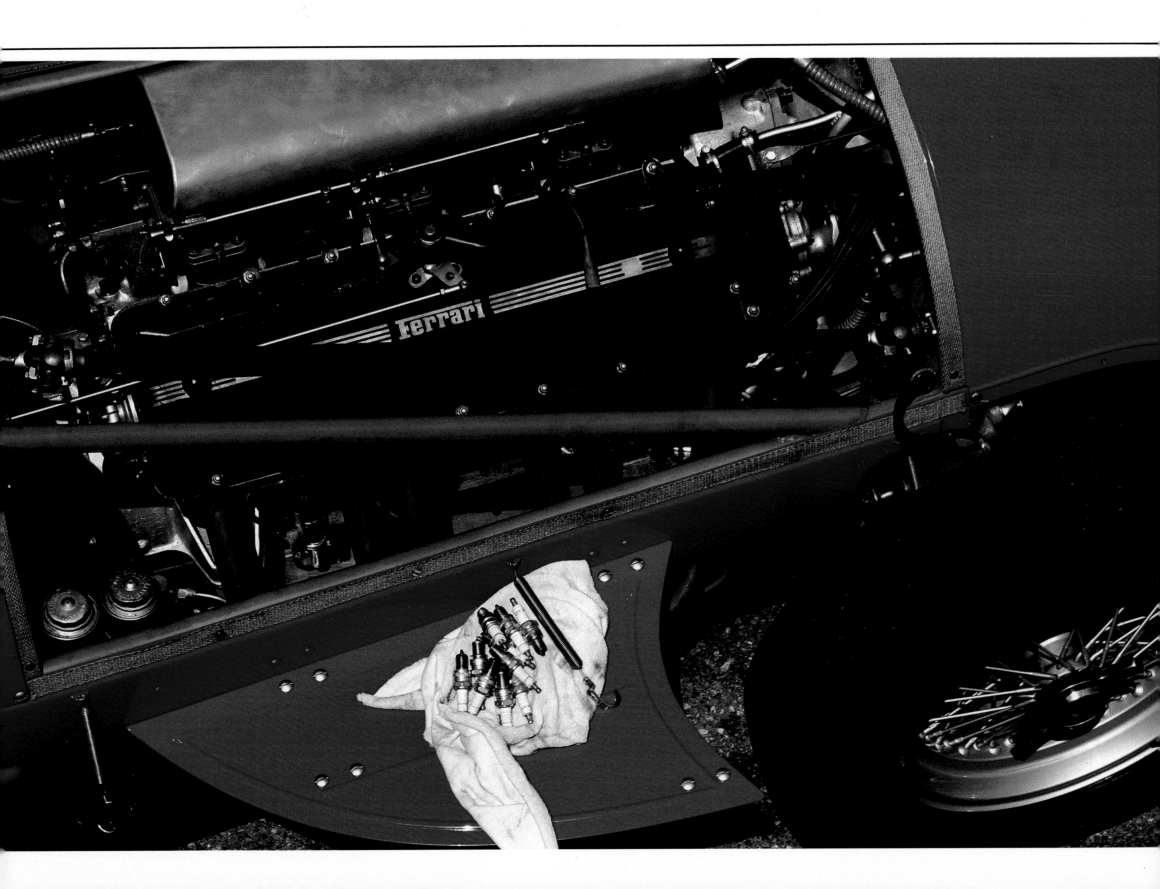

Four of the 375F1s, which were now limited to minor races, were modified to compete in the Indianapolis 500, and later sold after their unfortunate first official participation. The three other 375F1s went to Brazilian "Chico" Landi; British industrialist Tony Vandervell, Ferrari's supplier of bearings, who modified his into the *Thin Wall Special;* and French driver Louis Rosier.

With his vehicle repainted French blue, Rosier won two of the four races he entered in 1952 and 1953, after which he decided to transform it into a Sports racing car. Without touching the chassis and leaving the steering wheel in its central position, Ferrari coach-builder Scaglietti created an original curvaceous body which the Clermont-born driver tried out at the Buenos Aires 1,000 Kilometer race on January 24, 1954.

The hybrid "375 Sport" finished seventh, far behind the factory's 375MMs, which were making their debut. Next, the 375 Plus appeared, reducing still further Rosier's chances. After three more unsuccessful races, Rosier traded his 375 for a 750 Monza, which was at least a true Sports racing car.

With a new single-seater body, the 375 was sold to New Zealander Ron Roycroft, and pursued a long career in the southern hemisphere, protected from European innovations. It was Albert Obrist's idea to restore the original body to this surviving rarity, a testament to the early ventures of engineer Lampredi.

Louis Rosier ordered a single-seater from Scaglietti for Sports car racing.

From Formula 1 to the road

In 1954, Ferraris were powered by three families of engine. The four-cylinder created by Lampredi for the 1952 Formula 2 took part both in Formula 1 (2.5 liters) and in Sports racing (two liters and three liters). Lampredi's twelve-cylinder engine also came into play on two fronts: Sports racing and private motoring. In Sports racing, the short-stroke 4.5 liter engine of the 375 Mille Miglia was quickly followed by a 4.9 liter version of the long-stroke engine which powered the 375 Plus. As far as private vehicles were concerned, the 375 America had a watered-down version of the short-stroke 4.5 liter and the 250 Europa had the same engine modified into three liters. Finally—a timid resurgence of the Colombo group—a three-liter engine entered the private market and the GT market in the 250GT.

Ferrari entered three experimental berlinettas in the Le Mans twenty-four-hour race, two 340MMs with the 4.1 liter, while the third had a long-stroke V-12, derived directly from the 4.5 liter engine of the 1951 single-seaters, hidden beneath its identical 340MM Pinin Farina bodywork. Progressively developed from the three Pinin Farina berlinettas at the end of the 1953 season, the two 4.5 liter vehicles played a decisive role in winning Ferrari's first world Sports racing title. These three vehicles are also descended from the 375 Mille Miglia, which was to become the war horse of Scuderia Ferrari and—above all—of its clients.

The 375 Mille Miglia was in fact finalized for the last round of the 1953 world championship, the Carrera Panamericana. In the Mexican Road Race—twice the length of the Mille Miglia—the new Ferrari, driven by Umberto Maglioli, was gaining on the quick 3.3 liter Lancias when a tire burst, allowing the Turin rivals to take the first three places.

The 375MM was a fantastic Ferrari due first of all to its engine. The twelve cylinders and 4.5 liters had matured well. Beyond an extrapolation of the Formula 1 engine, it was now a brilliant blend of extreme grand prix performance and its Sports racing derivatives. The reduced 68 mm stroke of the first-generation engine had been retained while the bore was increased from 80 to 84 mm, resulting in a total capacity of 4522 cc, only slightly larger than the 4494 cc of the grand prix engine. Two magnetos provided ignition through twelve spark plugs; fuel was supplied by three four-choke 40 mm Webers. The 375MM had a little more than 300 horsepower (the catalog said 340), compared with 380 for the single-seater.

With the 375MM berlinetta, Pinin Farina reached the apex.

Car 0368 AM, the second of six beautiful 375MM berlinettas, was made in 1954 for French industrialist, Michel Paul-Cavallier.

The 375MM is better known as an open car, but is less exclusive in that version; Pinin Farina made twenty-two of them.

The grand prix engine had become usable on the road.

Coupled to a four-speed gearbox, the engine was mounted on an all-purpose and somewhat rustic base, directly inherited from the first barchettas of 1950. Transverse leaf springs at the front, rigid rear axle, shock absorbers with Houdaille shafts—nothing had changed, apart from the longer 2600 mm wheelbase. This layout must have been judged sufficient for a "competition-customer" model; in fact, Scuderia Ferrari was soon to abandon its 375MM to the customers. For its own needs, the racing team moved to the 375 Plus with its 4.9 liter engine and de Dion axle.

The 375MM's bodywork was sublime. The earlier work of Pinin Farina—on the 250MM and the three experimental berlinettas of 1953—appeared as rough prototypes compared with this Mexican berlinetta. The sharp angles were gone, the compartments harmonized and the details which had been improvised for racing were refined. This was Pinin Farina's first masterpiece, the archetype of Italian bodywork, able to win both races and the classiest Concours d'Elegance.

A beautiful work is usually reproduced to the point of ubiquity. Not the 375MM; only seven vehicles of its type were made.

Car number 0358 AM was the first 375MM berlinetta, which appeared at the 1953 Car-

For racing and Concours d'Elegance

rera driven by Maglioli. Sold not long afterward in Argentina, it was bought about ten years ago by a Canadian connoisseur, who has restored it to perfect condition.

The second, 0368 AM, the vehicle pictured here from the Mas du Clos, was made for French industrialist Michel Paul-Cavallier for use on the road. It was the second Ferrari owned by Paul-Cavallier, following a Ghia 340 America coupe. It may be noted that nothing distinguishes this "street" 375MM from a racing car.

The third, 0378 AM, was delivered for road use to a Sr. Wax, and was not the last exceptional Ferrari owned by this Genoese industrialist. Fenders and luxurious decorations gave this vehicle a more sophisticated character. Its present location is not known.

Definitely more of a Sports racing car, the fourth, 0380 AM, appeared at the 1954 Geneva

Three pairs of quadruple-choke carburetors and more than 300 horsepower.

Salon, and was sold to Count Baggio who, along with Porfirio Rubirosa, entered it in Le Mans and then, immediately afterward, in the sand at Tertre Rouge. The car has not resurfaced since the Le Mans practice in 1960, which it attended as an old, but unwrinkled spectator; not even the provisional number plate had changed.

Car 0416 AM was delivered painted in white, with fenders and laterally adjustable passenger seat, to a Roman who must have alternated between being affectionate and being cool. It has just arrived in Switzerland after having been cherished for more than twenty years by an American owner.

With its fenders and urbane finish, 0472 AM was packed up and sent to San Francisco for Alfred Ducato, an advertising executive. For the past ten years, it has belonged to an engineer in Detroit, who has given up a 250GTO to be able to devote himself to a masterful restoration of this red berlinetta with its black roof.

Presented on the Pinin Farina stand at the 1954 Turin Salon, the seventh and last 375MM berlinetta, 0490 AM, suffered from too prominent wings. The style was altered.

To these seven (or six) berlinettas, three other 375MMs of differing designs may be added. The star of the 1954 Paris Salon, 0456 AM was bought by film director Roberto Ros-

The 375MM promoted the name berlinetta for a whole line of famous Ferraris

sellini; it is another Pinin Farina masterpiece but in a completely different style. The car is currently being restored. A Ghia-designed coupe, 0476 AM, also had a strange elegance. Car number 0488 AM was a cabriolet owned by Belgian King Leopold.

One month after the Mexican Road Race, another 375MM made its (victorious) debut at the Casablanca twelve-hour race. The base was identical but, though still very beautiful, the open bodywork, which Pinin Farina was to repeat on twenty-two other copies, lacked the berlinetta's irresistible attraction.

From racing to royalty

On December 31, 1954, a strange chassis was delivered from Maranello to Pinin Farina's workshop. Despite its 2600 mm wheelbase, the chassis itself differed substantially from that of the 375 Mille Miglia, with which the Turin designer was well acquainted; Pinin Farina had dressed twenty-four 375MMs —eight berlinettas and sixteen spyders.

Several unusual characteristics were apparent on this chassis. First, the steering was no longer on the right, but on the left. Second, the classic transverse leaf spring suspension had been replaced by two helical springs which, combined with wishbones, made the front wheels independent. Finally, the chassis lacked the characteristic four-speed gearbox coupled to the differential and the de Dion rear axle.

In the engine, the magnetos might have been considered strange but the main mechanicals were less visible although just as unusual. This was no longer a 4.5 liter, but a 4.9 liter engine, the origin of which is worth explaining.

From the beginning of the 1954 season, Ferrari had abandoned the 375MM to its customers and had replaced it with the 375 Plus which, under its similar spyder body, hid an engine of almost five liters, no longer derived from the 4.5 liter engine of the 375MM but directly from the grand prix cars. The engine had a longer stroke of 74.5 instead of 68 mm; liners (still screwed on to the cylinder heads, according to the Lampredi method) gave a bore of 84 mm. Total capacity had increased to 4954 cc, and this dry-sump engine with its

Before the royal body, this unique chassis, with the steering wheel on the left and a 4.9 liter engine, was tried out around Maranello.

*An altimeter was among
the instruments for a king
who liked to be informed.*

three Weber 42 DCZs, put out 340 horsepower at 6500 rpm.

The engine was similar to the one which had just contributed to Ferrari's second world title by winning the 1954 Le Mans twenty-four-hours race, with Maurice Trintignant and Gonzales, and the Carrera Panamericana, with Maglioli. Such a favor could only be granted to a special customer. It revealed the esteem in which Commendatore Ferrari held King Leopold of Belgium, since it was for him that the car was destined.

In his book, *My Great Joys*, Enzo Ferrari described the monarch, who often came to visit him, in the following terms: "He seemed to me to be a man who would have made a good engineer, a man gifted in technique and who bitterly regretted not ever having been able to follow his inclination ... At the wheel, I found him courageous and able to confront danger with resolution and skill."

King Leopold evidently had an affirmed taste for beautiful cars. Before the war, he had

In 1969, 0488 AM came to Chicago, where it remains to this day.

a Bugatti equipped for the road and the Ferrari 342 America he received at the end of 1952 was only the first of several superb Ferraris delivered to the Palace of Laeken, as the Princess de Rethy seemed to share this royal passion.

On this unique chassis (0488 AM), Pinin Farina produced a cabriolet of historical

27

importance. Its innovative beauty was to set the trend for years to come. Was not the 250GT Spyder California inspired by it?

Several years later, Battista "Pinin" Farina described this cabriolet as "la fuoriserie che non invecchia"—the prototype that does not age. And yet, at the end of the sixties, this mobile monument, lost in a Brussels garage, appeared worn out. In August 1969, Wayne Gollomb, a young attorney from the Midwest,

came across an advertisement in *Car and Driver* and jumped on the first plane for Brussels. Several months later, the magnificent black cabriolet arrived in Chicago and has remained with the same owner ever since.

The restoration of this unique Ferrari took nearly ten years. Nothing can curb our admiration, not even the color chosen for the leather upholstery; according to several witnesses, the hide was originally beige.

The unusual rake of the windshield, the faired in headlights and the calm harmony of line suggest a renaissance of Italian style.

A superb failure

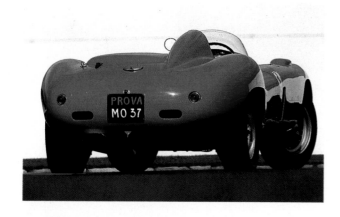

This design was attributed to Dino Ferrari; Scaglietti adopted it for the six-cylinder chassis.

Having converted the twelve-cylinder engine from 3.3 liters, 4.1 liters, 4.5 liters and then to nearly five liters, engineer Aurelio Lampredi turned his attention to a four-cylinder engine which, starting from two liters, would increase to 2.5 liters, three liters and 3.5 liters. Before concluding a seven-year career at Maranello with a two-cylinder engine of 2.5 liters, the person Enzo Ferrari described as "the most prolific engineer Ferrari has ever had," attempted to utilize the inline six formula. By coincidence, the six-cylinder experiment materialized at Ferrari in 1955, when all of its world championship rivals—Maserati, Jaguar and Aston Martin—were also concentrating on engines of this configuration. All, except Mercedes.

The six-cylinder engines brought out by Lampredi for Ferrari were in fact extrapolations of his inline four engine. The blocks, with fixed cylinder heads, double ignition and dry sump, in fact existed in many dimensions. The addition of two cylinders allowed infinite variations; Lampredi experimented with many of them. Still, only two six-cylinder engines were actually used in racing: the 118 and the 121.

The 118 was the first, its name corresponding to a number in the chronological order of Maranello engines. It was derived directly from the 625F1, the four-cylinder, 2.5 liter engine made for 1954 Formula 1 races. The 118 had different pistons to reduce the compression ratio from 11:1 to 8.75:1, allowing the use of normal fuel. Otherwise, the engine retained exactly the same configuration as the 625F1's 90 mm stroke and 94 mm bore. With two extra cylinders, this gave the 118 a total capacity of 3747.6 cc. Lubrication was provided by the classic dry sump with a tank set in the front right wing. With two Weber horizontal twin carburetors of 45 mm—compared

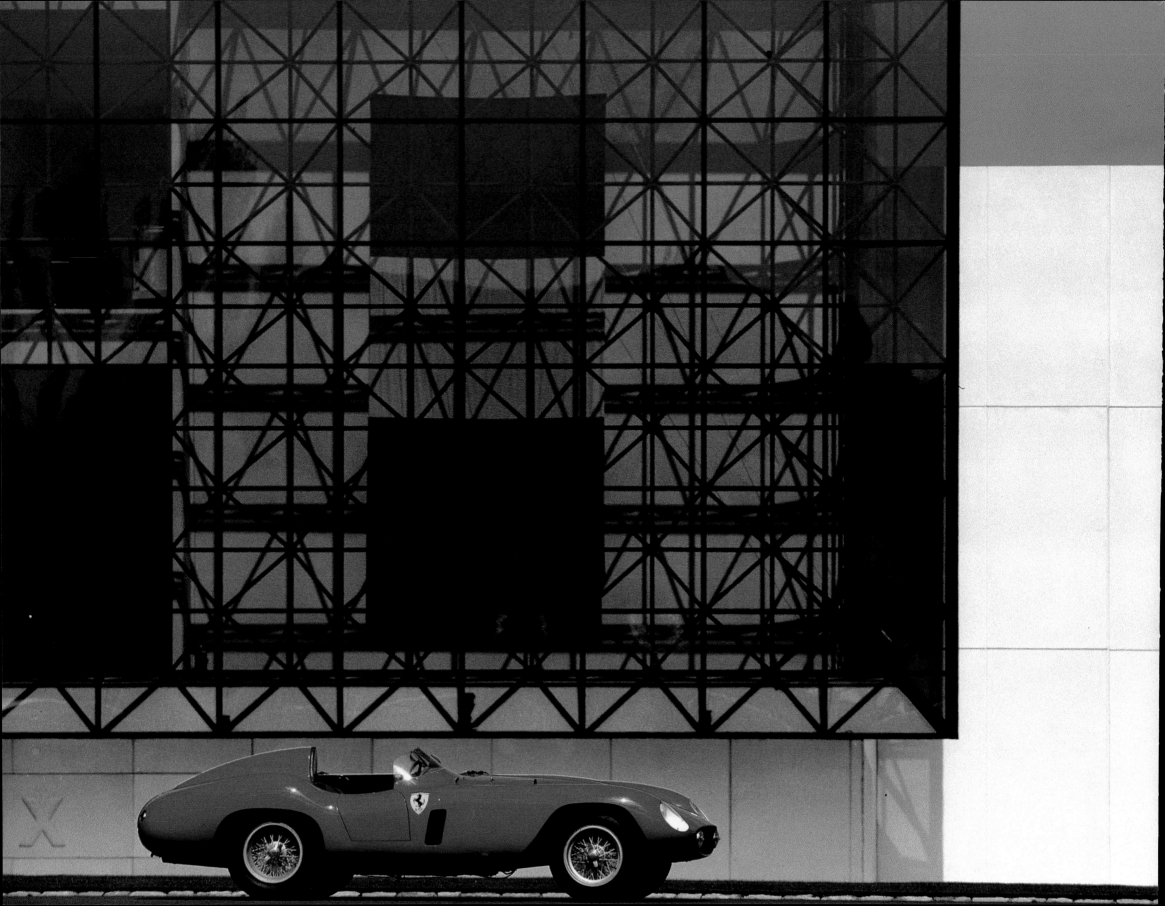

In 1955, Mercedes-Benz swept aside the opposition

with 50 mm for the Formula 1—the strength of this first six-cylinder engine was put at 310 horsepower at 6000 rpm.

A new chassis was not made to accommodate the 118 engine; the chassis from the four-cylinder Sports racing engine in the 500 Mondial and 750 Monza was elongated by 150 mm, providing a wheelbase of 2400 mm, although the track remained unchanged. This somewhat conservative base consisted of front suspension with wishbones and helical springs, a de Dion rear axle and a five-speed gearbox placed beside the differential. The equipage covered by beautiful two-seater, open bodywork made at Scaglietti. Legend attributes the design to Enzo Ferrari's son, Dino, and it had already been admired on the 500 Mondial and the 750 Monza.

The first round of the 1955 championship took place at Buenos Aires, where the unique 118—entered with the Gonzales/Trintignant team, who had won Le Mans six months earlier—was disqualified while in first place. With Piero Taruffi, the same 118 took its well-deserved revenge in the Targa Florio. This non-championship race was only a rehearsal to the 1955 Mille Miglia, where a strong Mercedes team of four 300SLRs was expected. For the race, Lampredi unveiled a new version of a four-cylinder, 2.9 liter engine which, with two extra cylinders, had a capacity of 4412 cc. With the help of three 50 mm carburetors, the 121 engine put out 330 horsepower with more torque.

Four 121s were at the Mille Miglia starting line in Brescia, driven by Taruffi, Maglioli, Paolo Marzoto and Eugenio Castelotti. Castelotti was the only one to complete the circuit, yet he only came in third, behind two Mercedes.

Umberto Maglioli and the 121 of our photographs, number 0558, at the 1955 Le Mans twenty-four-hour race.

A piquant anecdote is provided by the experience of the three surviving drivers revealed by Gianni Marzotto in his history of the Mille Miglia. As he no doubt considered the three-liter Mercedes to be supreme, Enzo Ferrari preferred to keep secret the engine capacity of his new 121s. They were officially announced as 3.8 liters.

At Le Mans, the three 121s driven by Maglioli/Phil Hill, Castelotti/Marzotto and Trintignant/Harry Schell made an impression but without success; none crossed the finish line. Mike Hawthorn, whose Jaguar won after the Mercedes' withdrawal, recorded this memory of the 121s: "The Ferraris did not have as good brakes as we did and their road holding on bends was not as good as it might have been; but when accelerating, Castelotti left us both standing, leaving an incredible trail of black rubber on the track as he disappeared in a roar."

For the other rounds of the championship, Ferrari brought out his four-cylinder, three-liter and 4.5 liter, engines but at the Swedish Grand Prix, a non-championship Sports event, Castelotti brought in the only 121 entered in third position, behind the 300SLRs driven by Fangio and Stirling Moss.

Scaglietti was the first to adapt the streamlined single-seater headrest to Sports racing cars

This was to be the last official race of the Lampredi six-cylinder engine. The five cars were sold to private American stables, after only five appearances that were often brief but always impressive.

The example photographed near Paris, 0558 LM, is one of the four 121s that followed the single and unique 118, 0484 LM. It is the vehicle that was driven by Maglioli and Hill at Le Mans and probably also by Castelotti at the 1,000 Mile Sports Car Grand Prix in Sweden.

Weapon for a battle that never took place

▬

In 1955, Mercedes-Benz ruled supreme. In an attempt to unseat Mercedes, Scuderia Ferrari made the best of what it had and Lampredi's latest ideas were thrown desperately into battle. Thus there were the vain attempts of the four-cylinder, three-liter engined 750 Monza and the 3.5 liter 875 Sport as well as the six-cylinder, 3.8 liter 118 and the 4.4 liter 121. A final assault with the return of the twelve-cylinder engine never took place.

In 1955 a Mercedes crashed into the crowd at Le Mans and the number of casualties was horrific. This accident also had a negative effect on motor racing. In some countries, such as Switzerland, races were simply forbidden, while elsewhere, some events were called off, suspended or postponed. In Mexico, the great Carrera was canceled.

The Mexican Road Race was about to take place for the fifth time, completing the 1955 manufacturers' world championship. Ferrari could only hope for a gallant last stand, but a vehicle was nevertheless prepared especially for this event, and two copies—at least—were ready when the race's cancelation was confirmed.

For this 3,000 kilometer race in which speed and stamina took precedence over all other factors, Ferrari staked everything on power and Lampredi produced the largest engine that had ever been made at Maranello. Leaving to one side the 4.9 liter engine of the 375 Plus, which was already two years old, he started with another 4.9 liter, the one he had just conceived for the production 410 Superamerica. In fact, this V-12 engine had a similar capacity—4961 cc compared with 4954 cc for the 375 Plus—but had the advantage of a shorter stroke, 68 mm instead of 74.5. The existing block was topped with cylinder heads with double ignition derived from those of the last 375F1s but with four distributors mounted in pairs behind each of the two camshafts. Fuel was routed through a battery of three quadruple Weber 42 DCZ/4 carburetors. The wet sump of the private model gave way to a dry sump accompanied by a tank in the front left wing. With a reasonable compression ratio of 9:1, the horsepower was 380 at 7000 rpm.

The 410 Sport is thus a rare example in Ferrari's history of a racing engine evolving from a motoring engine. Following Tipo 126,

Designed for the canceled Carrera Panamericana, 0596 CM only competed in one race for Ferrari—the 1956 Buenos Aires 1,000 Kilometer, driven by Fangio and Castelotti, seen here at the wheel.

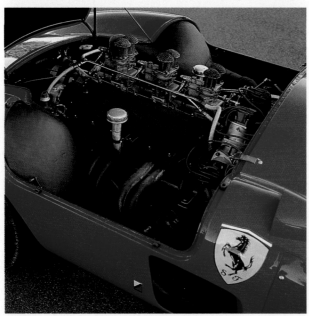

the racing engine, Tipo 126C, was installed on a chassis that was slightly shorter—with a wheelbase of 2350 mm—and lighter than that of the preceding six-cylinder engines, yet still of similar configuration. In fact, the new chassis used the former's front suspension with wishbones, helical springs and Houdaille shock absorbers, and the de Dion rear axle flanked by four torque rods and four lever arm shock absorbers of the same type. The axle-mounted gearbox, however, only had four ratios.

From a design whose origin is not known with certainty, but to which Pinin Farina was probably no stranger, Scaglietti made three beautiful aluminum bodies, recognizable by their hoods which overlapped onto the front wings. This larger opening was intended to facilitate access to the twelve additional spark plugs which were placed between the exhaust ports.

Two vehicles, 0596 CM and 0598 CM, were hastily named 410 Sport, because of their cylinder capacity, but the suffix CM on their chassis numbers confirmed their intended destination: Carrera Messicana, Italian for the defunct Mexican Road Race.

A stallion in the Mas du Clos stable

Deprived of their initial objective, the two beauties nevertheless appeared at the Buenos Aires 1,000 Kilometer race on January 29, for the first round of the 1956 world championship. On this fast circuit, formed largely of 9.5 kilometers of highway, 0598 CM even had the honor of making its debut with "campionissimo" Fangio, who joined the Ferrari team after the withdrawal of Mercedes. Fangio was assisted by Castelotti, while Luigi Musso and Peter Collins were the team for 0596 CM. On the hood of 0596 CM two bulges showed that for the occasion the two additional distributors had been mounted in front of the camshafts.

Fangio immediately took the lead, followed by Musso, Moss' three-liter Maserati, and Olivier Gendebien and Hill's 3.5 liter Ferrari. On the thirty-fifth lap, Castelotti took over from Fangio in the leading vehicle but ran into a bale of straw and burst a tire, ceding the lead to Collins until, in the sixty-first lap, 0596 CM's differential gave way. Fangio had by then made up for lost time and was struggling for first place with Moss. When 0598 CM's transmission failed, the Maserati was victorious. Gendebien and Hill, who came in second in their 857 Sport entered by Luigi Chinetti, salvaged Ferrari's honor.

This first sortie was also the last for the 410 Sport with Scuderia Ferrari; they were immediately sold. Car 0598 CM went to American John Edgar, and has remained in the United States, where it won several races, in particular with Carrol Shelby, Ritchie Ginther and Masten Gregory.

Car 0596 CM, the vehicle in our photo-

"Campionissimo" Fangio raced it first

graphs, started a second, somewhat anonymous career with Swede, Sturre Nottorp. In 1960, after a two-year comeback in the United States, it appeared in an advertisement in *Road & Track* for the sum of $9,000! Since 1972, it has been in good company in the Mas du Clos collection. The four distributors have been restored to their original position, and the welding inside the hood is evidence of its experience in Buenos Aires.

Lone knight

Ferrari prepared two 410 Sports for the Carrera Panamericana. Yet before making the two twin-ignition barchettas, Ferrari had already made two other 410 Sports, chassis numbers 0592 CM and 0594 CM.

Little is known of the first car. It probably served as a factory prototype before going to American Tony Parravano with a Scaglietti body lowered to such a point that the air inlet for the carburetors formed an even more pronounced projection on the hood. The front was also equipped with an oval radiator grille, a detail that was apparently dear to Parravano, since it was found on all the special Ferraris and Maseratis in his stable before his sudden death.

The second car, 0594 CM, was given, also by Scaglietti, a two-seater body, although closed this time. Starting from the design that Pinin Farina had just created for the 250GT berlinettas, the Modena carrozzeria included an interesting adaptation with a wheelbase that was 250 mm shorter, causing a total rebalancing of the original design. The long Lampredi V-12, despite the fact that the gearbox had been transferred to the back, obliged Scaglietti to move the cockpit considerably. The result-

ing squat appearance made the vehicle look even more aggressive.

The technical characteristics of this berlinetta were similar to those of the three other 410 Sports: a chassis with 2350 mm wheelbase, independent front suspension, a four-speed gearbox coupled to the differential and a de Dion axle. The engine block was the same 4.9 liter short-stroke from the 410 Superamerica production car, complete with a dry sump and a separate oil tank. The ventilation scoop on the front left wing of the berlinetta shows that this tank was set as far forward as possible, to provide extra space in the cramped cockpit. On the other hand, like the prototype sold to Parravano and unlike the two barchettas that followed, the ignition used only twelve spark plugs. Car 0594 CM's horsepower was less than 380.

Was this berlinetta, like the two twin-ignition barchettas that followed it, designed specifically for the Carrera? This hypothesis has never been put forward. In a race as unpredictable as the Carrera, a team of three vehicles would have made sense. Moreover, a berlinetta, even if not as light and elaborate as the two barchettas, would, if necessary, have been

On the open road at Mas du Clos; the most powerful berlinetta sold in the fifties.

capable of carrying out the role of substitute. In 1951, Ferrari won the Mexican race with two 212 coupes; in 1951, three 340 berlinettas battled vainly with the 300SL Mercedes; and in 1954, Ferrari employed no less than four 375s with closed bodies to combat the Lancia offensive. Mercedes also prepared two 300SLRs with closed bodywork for the 1955 Carrera Panamericana.

The fact remains that the race was canceled and that Ferrari had to reclassify two, three or four of its vehicles which had been deprived of their purpose. The superb and unique berlinetta was delivered—we might even say "awarded"—to a person with close links to Ferrari, Michel Paul-Cavallier. The Nancy, France, industrialist's 375MM berlinetta, of which we have already spoken, was therefore replaced by 0594 CM.

In its time, this 410 berlinetta was certainly the most powerful Ferrari ever sold for use on the road. Enzo Ferrari had it suitably decorated for his friend. With exceptional care, Scaglietti painted it "rosso corsa," a red that was slightly darker than the usual red of

For a personal friend of Enzo Ferrari

today's Ferraris and quite unusual for a private Ferrari vehicle. Inside, a tachometer was added to the dashboard and the whole was upholstered with luxurious French blue leather.

As if by magic, this legendary 410 Sport has now rejoined, in the Mas du Clos collection, its precursor, the 375MM berlinetta and one of its sisters, the 410 Sport barchetta which was driven by Musso and Collins at Buenos Aires.

There is a true family likeness with the contemporary 250GT.

No speedometer had been planned for the racing version.

For the road version, three twin-choke carburetors and twelve spark plugs only.

The long race

The spectacle of red Sports racing and Formula 1 cars being dominated, as they were in 1955, by Mercedes, dismayed not only Maserati, Lancia and Ferrari, but the whole of Italy. What is more, when Scuderia Lancia, after a truly remarkable effort, announced its withdrawal, the disaster became almost political; a regrouping of forces was decided upon in high places. The result was a ceremony at Turin on July 26, 1955, during which Lancia handed over all its Formula 1 material to Ferrari, including six single-seater D50s and great quantities of projects, studies and plans. The Commendatore's comment—"A wonderful gesture of solidarity and understanding"—was recorded later.

Ferrari's situation was in fact critical. There had been a long succession of sporting failures without hope in sight, and sales of both Sports racing and private cars fell to below 100 units per year.

An important contribution from the Lancia heritage was the arrival at Ferrari, in the capacity of consultant, of Vittorio Jano, the creator of the Lancia D50 and one of the most brilliant engineers in the automobile world. After seven prolific years of service, Lampredi left Ferrari for Fiat, and the Maranello team was reformed around three men: engineers Andrea Fraschetti, Luigi Bellentani and Alberto Massimino. Bellentani returned to Ferrari after having been technical director at Maserati from 1946 to 1952. With young Fraschetti and under the guidance of Jano, he concerned himself with the engines. Massimino, who had participated with Colombo in the creation of the Alfa Romeo Alfetta and with Bellentani in the development of the 815, took charge of chassis work.

The new Maranello team set to work to recast the Lancia D50 as a Ferrari Sports racing car for Formula 1 racing. They also hedged their bets by creating a new twelve-cylinder, the 290MM, and by continuing to develop two four-cylinder engines. This development of the Lampredi engines produced two vehicles for

The 1956 Sebring twelve-hour race. Eugenio Castelotti and 0802 head for a first victory.

A proven engine beneath a fresh but refined body.

the 1956 season: the 500 Testa Rossa, which was intended for customers; and the 860 Monza, for Scuderia Ferrari.

The 860 Monza was a combination of a tried and tested engine with a new chassis—the adaptation of a four-cylinder engine to a chassis intended for the 290MM. The intention was probably to counter possible immature faults in the new V-12. This four-cylinder, 3.5 liter engine had indeed already been tested during the 1955 season on the 750 Monza. It kept the salient features of the Lampredi engines— blind-end cylinder heads, two overhead camshafts and twin ignition—but was original in that its 102 mm bore was smaller than its 105 mm stroke. This resulted in a capacity of 3432 cc and distinguished it as both the largest four-cylinder and the only long-stroke engine ever produced at Maranello. It produced nearly 310 horsepower at 6200 rpm, about thirty more than its three-liter predecessor with the same Weber horizontal twin 58 DCOA/3 carburetors and the same 8.5:1 compression ratio.

The chassis, Tipo 520, that carried this engine differed from the 519C of the preceding 410 Sport mainly in the addition of a trellis of

The largest four-cylinder engine ever produced at Maranello

tubes doubling the two main side frames. Other items were also retained: the 2350 mm wheelbase, the wishbones and helical springs at the front and, at the back, the de Dion axle and axle-mounted four-speed gearbox, which was probably less tested by the more modest power of the new 3.5 liter engines.

Scaglietti covered the 1956 3.5 liter 290MM and 860 Monza with bodywork that was identical, apart from the boss on the hood, which was distinctly flatter on the four-liter car. The design is not foreign to that of the two last 410 Sport barchettas, which suggests once more

that Pinin Farina may have made a contribution.

Six 3.5 liter vehicles—four- and twelve-cylinders—were made and used by Scuderia Ferrari during the 1956 season. They carried chassis numbers 0602, 0604, 0606, 0616, 0626 and 0628, but their individual stories have to this day remained vague and the interchangeability of the engines makes their histories foggier.

By chance, the 860 Monza (0602) from the Musee de l'Automobiliste, photographed here, has had a clear and brilliant—although short—history. Piloted by Fangio and Castelotti, the 860 Monza won the Sebring twelve-hour race. Immediately after this success in the second round of the 1956 championship, 0802 was sold to John von Neumann, the wealthy importer of Volkswagen Beetles into the United States. One month after being honored at Sebring, 0802 reappeared on the wooded and tortured circuit of Pebble Beach, California. A fuel tank set behind the driver's head to stabilize the vehicle for short circuits, a shorter axle

Fangio preferred it to the twelve-cylinder engine

ratio and a new coat of red paint were not enough, however, to allow Phil Hill to come in better than second, behind Carroll Shelby and the three-liter 750 Monza with which Hill had won the same Del Monte Trophy the year before. Car 0802 then took an early and quiet retirement, which explains its perfect original condition.

Fangio's bathtub

Car 0626 in the colors of Argentina. Fangio in the Mille Miglia, then with Phil Hill at the Nurburgring.

After the failure of the 410 Sport at Buenos Aires and the success at Sebring with the 860 Monza, the great Fangio was exempted from the Targa Florio. The Sicilian race was a non-championship event, but one to which Ferrari and the Italian manufacturers attached great importance, both for training before the ritual Mille Miglia and for the popular interest aroused by this extravagant race with its 1,000 bends. The Targa Florio is also where the 290MMs received their baptism of fire—but without success, since neither Castelotti nor Musso, the two Italian hopefuls of the Scuderia, were able to make the finish. Victory on that day went to a third official Ferrari, an elderly four-cylinder, 3.5 liter vehicle from the previous season, allocated to Peter Collins and his navigator, photographer Louis Klemantaski.

Fangio thus avoided the first road race of the 1956 season but he did not miss the second, the Mille Miglia. It is interesting to note that the renowned Argentine was as lukewarm toward road races as he was enthusiastic about Formula 1 Grand Prix races. The 290MM allocated to him for the great tour of Italy reinforced his feelings—although a similar car eventually won the race. "If I had ever wondered what it was like to race in a bathtub, I would now find out," he complained at the end of the 1,600 kilometers covered at speeds of nearly 130 km/h on wet roads. He cursed the mechanics who had made a ventilation hole in the vehicle which only served to soak him each time he used the brakes. Fangio and his "bathtub" nevertheless came in fourth behind Castelotti, the winner in a 290MM that was similar but had a yellow nose; Collins and Klemantaski, in a 860 Monza with a green nose; and Musso in another 860 Monza with a yellow nose.

The 290MM number 0626 pictured here is the Ferrari with the "Argentine nose" that Fangio entered in the Mille Miglia on April 29, 1956. Claude Vialard, historian of the Mas du Clos collection, has carefully restored this nasal stylishness.

The 290MM was thus the first Sports racing Ferrari truly designed by the new Maranello team. The V-12, Tipo 130, marked the start of a new era, although some traits characteristic of Colombo or Lampredi were still to be found

An adjustable wind deflector or Brooklands screen protected the frail regulation streamlining.

in its mechanics. Lampredi's technique of a cylinder/ cylinder-head monoblock with wet liners screwed on was retained but the novel dimensions were the first indications of a new design. The fairly short stroke was 69.5 mm and the bore 73 mm, giving a cylinder capacity of 290 cc (which also gave the model its name) and a total capacity of 3490.6 cc, very close to that of the contemporary four-cylinder engine. From five liters, the V-12 had gone back to 3.5 liters, another new philosophy.

The V-12 Tipo 130 is shorter but wider than its predecessor, and this is noticeable on the two cylinder head covers. The distribution with the dual camshafts was retained—temporarily. A great deal of work, however, had

The end of 0626's career at Buenos Aires.

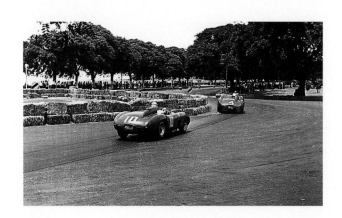

gone into the combustion chambers to perfect the induction, exhaust and ignition. The diameter of the inlet valve was 35 mm while the exhaust valve was 29 mm, an increase of more than twenty percent for the inlet and ten percent for the exhaust.

In these cylinder heads, twin spark plugs fired each cylinder and four distributors, as on the 410 Sport, were mounted behind the camshafts. Two different types of carburetor were used in the course of the season to supply the twelve induction pipes via a water-cooled manifold: three 40 mm twins or three 36 mm quadruples, depending on circumstances. In the second case, the new V-12 put out 320 horsepower at 7300 rpm.

The chassis, Tipo 520, was common to the 290MM and the 860 Monza, as was the body—apart from the hood, which, on the twelve-cylinder engine, had a tall cold-air inlet and a bulbous boss above the carburetors.

The six 3.5 liters, both four- and twelve-cylinder engines, shared the honor of bringing Ferrari its third world title at the end of the 1956 Sports racing championship. Yet despite their similarities, the two models behaved differently. This was due not to their balance or power—the 290MM had between ten and twenty horsepower on the 860 Monza—but to another reason, their engines. The large four-cylinder, long-stroke engine had considerable inertia, whereas, when decelerating, the very

"electric" over-square twelve-cylinder engine hardly slowed the 290MM at all. Passing from one vehicle to the other left several drivers with everlasting memories.

Fangio did not let himself be taken in, however. His position as first driver gave him the privilege of choosing his vehicle. Indeed, apart from the 1956 Mille Miglia, the world champion always drove the 860 Monza. Understandably, he preferred it on hilly circuits such as the Nurburgring where, with Castelotti, he finished second behind the 300S Maserati of "Ringmeister" Stirling Moss. Fangio also chose the 860 Monza on fast circuits such as Kristianstadt, where, in the Swedish Grand Prix, the last event of the 1956 championship, a mechanical fault in the last laps forced him to cede first place to the 290MM driven by Hill and Trintignant.

The "Argentine" 290MM (0626) thus experienced the honor and rage of the great champion only once. At the Nurburgring it finished third with Hill and Ken Wharton, and in Sweden, Count Wolfgang von Trips and Collins brought it home to second place. It finally took its revenge on the rapid Buenos Aires circuit by winning—after the withdrawal of Fangio's Maserati—the first round of the 1957 championship. It was driven by Masten Gregory, Castelotti and Musso, and had perhaps been equipped for the occasion with the new four-camshaft engine. But that is another story.

Cafe racer

Pinin Farina began working for Ferrari in 1951; the collaboration grew intimate over the years. The coachbuilder at 107 Corso Trapani in Turin was allocated Ferrari chassis with increasing regularity in what became an almost exclusive arrangement. Pinin Farina's keenest competitors—Touring-Superleggera, Vignale and Ghia—were inevitably ousted one after the other.

The fact that Pinin Farina's dominance at Ferrari did not become a monopoly was certainly because both Enzo Ferrari and Battista "Pinin" Farina, as sensible administrators of autonomous enterprises, knew they could not accept such interdependence. In 1957, two other bodyworkers thus shared with Pinin Farina the task of covering the Ferrari chassis: Scaglietti and Boano. Sergio Scaglietti's small workshop at Modena was mostly assigned racing models. As for Carrozzeria Boano, recently founded in Turin by Mario Felice Boano and Luciano Pollo, two Ghia renegades, it provided the bodywork for the small-scale manufacture of the 250GT coupe from 1956 onward. Yet these two establishments rarely produced their own designs; they primarily transcribed into sheet metal ideas that came from Pinin Farina.

There were no hard and fast rules, and exceptions often occurred. One of Boano's creations was thus shown at the Geneva Salon in March 1956 in the form of a surprising cabriolet. The car was constructed on the 250GT chassis with its 2600 mm wheelbase.

The first 250GT convertible was this comfortable cabriolet signed by Boano.

Pinin Farina treated the cabriolet theme in a more racing car style and avoided the fashion for fins. Its first exercise was this spyder with its indented left-hand door, which Peter Collins equipped with Dunlop disc brakes and wheels.

The chassis had until then only been used for the Pinin Farina/Boano coupe and the Pinin Farina/Scaglietti berlinetta.

The result was a little tortured, but thanks are due to Boano's initiative in reviving the cabriolet theme, which Ferrari seemed to have forgotten for several years. The reaction of Pinin Farina took a year to arrive, but at the following Geneva Salon, the result was none the less surprising with its low lines, its fold-away top completely hidden behind the two bucket seats, its lack of side windows and its left door which was indented for the driver's elbow, in the grand sport style.

This strange "cafe racer" (0655 GT), which might well have remained a one-off show car like many others, in fact played two important roles in Ferrari's history. It had the honor of becoming the personal Ferrari of Peter Collins, who equipped it with disc brakes and Dunlop alloy wheels, like the D-type Jaguars. Legend has it that Maranello took a close interest in this experiment and that this brilliant Scuderia driver's initiative was not unconnected with Ferrari's abandonment of the ever-present drum brake: on the single-seaters at the end of the 1958 season; on the Testa Rossas at the beginning of the 1959 season; and on the 250GT berlinetta at the end of the same year, 1959.

But in March 1957, drum brakes reigned and convertible Ferraris were reborn. After only two months, a second and no less surprising convertible 250GT left the Corso Trapani workshops. Its lines were similar but its details were stranger still: the windshield was followed by a plexiglass apron which was continued on the doors; to benefit the driver without disturbing the airflow, the headrest was lengthened by a streamlined section above the trunk. This strange cafe racer, which has been rediscovered today (0663 GT), was delivered to the Belgian driver, Leon Dernier, but they were evidently never seen together on a circuit.

Intended for another Belgian, Andre Meert, the following project repeated lines of the same shape, but with infinitely more realism. This cabriolet (0705 GT) was in fact a repetition of the previous design in all its purity, but had a real windshield and wind-up side windows. The dimensions of the air inlet on the hood were reduced—in length and width—and a surrounding fender replaced the two rubber buffers at the rear while retaining their function at the front.

Meert has precise memories of this exceptional cabriolet and the paint that was applied to it following his directions: a deep bluish red that was so pigmented that it left a mark at the slightest contact. The interior was covered with light beige Connolly leather and the Borrani wheels had the novel feature of black-lacquered spokes, making the polished aluminum rims all the more shiny.

The wind in your hair

Peter Collins' spyder was followed by this "cafe racer" which heralded definite lines.

The 250GT cabriolet acquired all its splendor with this last prototype delivered to Belgium.

Andre Meert's cabriolet was followed by a batch of thirty-seven copies between 1957 and 1958 from the venerable workshops of the Corso Trapani. These 250GT cabriolets were among the last built by Pinin Farina before the coachbuilder moved to a new factory at Grugliasco on the outskirts of Turin.

Fortunately, no one asked for or was granted an alteration to the elegant cabriolet's lines. On the other hand, the finishing touches varied from one vehicle to another, in a multitude of details, personalized according to the tastes of the customer. Thus the dashboard could be covered with leather or lacquered with vermiculated paint. Fender vents with polished aluminum ornaments which appeared on the sides of Meert's prototype were only added to some of the vehicles. Several of them received a surrounding front fender instead of the two small vertical buffers, a tendency which be-

came more common on the last twenty or so cars of the batch. In this case, the large Marchal foglights were moved behind the radiator grille.

The upholstery and paint naturally presented the largest variance. For most of the Ferraris of this period, the leather worked by Pinin Farina came from Connolly in England and the paint from Max Meyer in Milan. The latter offered metallic varnishes, under the name of Lunalchrom and made from ground fish scales, that were of inimitable quality.

In 1957, the 250GT was in its third year. Constant technical development—the result of advances tested by the Scaglietti berlinettas in competitions—had expunged its earlier faults. With the 508C version of the traditional 250GT chassis, the front suspension with transverse leaf spring and the disconcerting steering were avoided but it was still necessary

to make do with the ancient shock absorbers with Houdaille arms and the (superb) brake drums.

The three-liter V-12 engine, Tipo 128C, retained the spark plugs in the middle of the Vee and under the three twin Weber 36 DCL carburetors, but the 240 horsepower attributed to it in the catalog was certainly optimistic. Still, the four-speed gearbox was new, unlike that of the three prototypes. It now benefited from a central stick, a normal H-shaped gate (with first at the top left) and, above all, Porsche synchromesh.

In fact, the mechanical specifications of these cabriolets, similar to the contemporary Boano coupes, were closely related to those of the first berlinettas of 1957; the fact that their

In 1959, Pininfarina changed style (and name), but the reputation increased.

road behavior differs is due largely to the contrast in weight. Whereas Scaglietti used aluminum sheets that were as thin as possible for racing cars, painted them with as few coats as possible and kept ornaments to the minimum, Pinin Farina covered the carbriolet with fairly thick sheets of steel so as to obtain the finish that is expected of a luxury car. This produced, for example, the door locks with their deep, precise sonority synonymous with quality. Several layers of paint on a well-prepared surface, suitable trimmings and the steel-framed top added an additional 400 lb. to the carbriolet. This stoutness manifested itself not only in the actual performance but in other areas of the car's behavior as well.

Moreover, while the racing berlinetta never stopped evolving—not including the "favors" granted to certain racing customers—the cabriolet remained fixed in its original mechanical configuration throughout its three-year lifespan. Maranello also did not agree to any significant customer requests with regard to the mechanics of these refined vehicles, apart from making two of them right-hand drive: one (0811 GT) delivered to Johannesburg, South Africa, the other (0921 GT) to Hong Kong.

Pictured here is the cabriolet that was painted a slightly garish sulphur yellow for an

Urbane charm inviting escape

Italian in Johannesburg. It is understandable that its present-day owner has departed from the rules of origin by painting it a metallic gray, thereby restoring a great Pinin Farina design to its true glory.

In 1960, a second series of cabriolets was launched with visible headlights, a more rectangular trunk and a squarer general outline. Its success increased, but its spirit had changed.

Chateau Ferrari 1957

Like great wine, Ferrari has its own sumptuous vintages. With its 335 Sports, its 250GT cabriolets and its 500TRCs, 1957 is one such vintage and, at the Turin Salon in November, it was crowned by a fabulous project by Pinin Farina on the non-racing 410 Superamerica chassis, number 0719 SA. The car was titled the 4.9 Superfast.

To explain this Americanism, we must go back one year. The name Superfast in fact came into being at the 1956 Paris Salon where Pinin Farina presented a unique and premonitory project—a real and extremely rare dream car in the Italian style. Its wide, low radiator grille, streamlined headlights, decorative molding with a middle line dividing two tones of paint—white on top and pale green below—its fenders which had been reduced to four buffers and its perfectly curved rear made it look impressively modern. The roof's cantilevered mounting eliminated windshield pillars, adding still more to the dream in an era when the dream car could only be American. The Americanism here is restricted to the name and also to two concave tailfins that spoiled the dream a bit.

Before being sold, the Superfast regained the windshield pillars. With its V-12 4.9 liter engine, twin-ignition and 350 horsepower, the Superfast lived up to its name.

For the Superfast of the 1957 Turin Salon, Pinin Farina selected the best discoveries from its first dream car and eliminated some of the more unrealistic details. Thus the blunt tailfins gave way to wings that flowed from front to back without obstacle and finished with two red lights streamlined like the headlights. The roof repeated the earlier design, with three inlets on each rear side panel, but the windshield had been masterfully integrated with its pillars. The chromium-plated trim surrounding the body disappeared, but a discrete fold produced the same effect. Finally, to protect the beautiful rear from bumps, a thin strip replaced the buffers. The 4.9 Superfast thus appeared to be longer and more slender than its precursor, when in fact it was shorter by 120 mm and taller by 50 mm!

To construct this monument, Pinin Farina used the base from the 410 Superamerica in its version with the wheelbase shortened from 2800 to 2600 mm. In the end, the Tipo 514

The evolution of Pinin Farina's style: the Superfast, the first of its name at the 1956 Paris Salon, a repeat of the 4.9 Superfast on a 250GT chassis; the 410 produced in 1958 and 1959.

chassis was closely related to that of the contemporary 250GT. Although it had the usual helical springs at the front, longitudinal leaves at the back and Houdaille shock absorbers with arms on the four wheels underneath, it could still be immediately distinguished from the 250GT by its track, which was 130 mm wider.

The Tipo 126 engine was the large oversquare V-12 with blind-end cylinder heads whose capacity had reached its maximum. The 4963 cc is in fact a record, since the Testa Rossa of today only amounts to 4943 cc. Supplied by three twin 42 mm Webers, instead of the standard 40 mm carburetors, the engine must have produced 350 horsepower; it did not beat the power record established by the 410 Sport berlinetta delivered to Michel Paul-Cavallier in 1956.

After the Turin Salon, this unique coupe was delivered to Jan de Vroom, a young American whose Dutch origin had given him a patronym suited to his passion: he was, along with Luigi Chinetti, one of the pillars of the North American Racing Team. The monthly *Sports Cars Illustrated*, which had the honor of submitting the 4.9 Superfast to a test drive, recorded a quarter-mile standing start in 13.9 seconds, compared with 16.1 seconds in a 250GT tested previously—another record.

The 4.9 Superfast's bodywork was repeated for Prince Bernhard of the Netherlands. The

Unique specimen for an American pioneer

copy was not far from equaling the original, but the narrower wheel track of the Prince's 250GT (0725 GT) chassis disturbed the balance.

The fact that the 4.9 Superfast was made on the penultimate Tipo 126 chassis might suggest that Pinin Farina nursed the hope of influencing Ferrari in his choice of body for the replacement model. Was this hope disappointed? The 410 Superamerica Series III was covered with another creation by the same designer. Greg Garrison, the only person today able to savor the delights of this specimen from the 1957 vintage, is not upset by this.

A fitting end for the four-cylinder engine

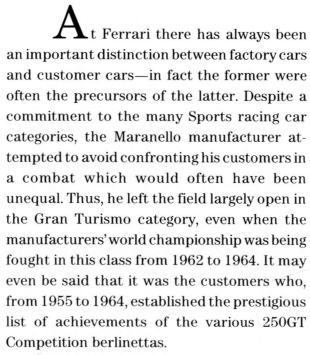

At Ferrari there has always been an important distinction between factory cars and customer cars—in fact the former were often the precursors of the latter. Despite a commitment to the many Sports racing car categories, the Maranello manufacturer attempted to avoid confronting his customers in a combat which would often have been unequal. Thus, he left the field largely open in the Gran Turismo category, even when the manufacturers' world championship was being fought in this class from 1962 to 1964. It may even be said that it was the customers who, from 1955 to 1964, established the prestigious list of achievements of the various 250GT Competition berlinettas.

Another class highly prized by private stables, especially in Italy, was the one reserved for Sports racing cars with a capacity under two liters. Even when, under the aegis of the engineer Lampredi, the capacity of Ferrari engines reached their zenith, Ferrari did not

forget its customers, who were often amateurs yet still contributed to the marque's success. Thus, in 1953, when the twelve-cylinder, two-liter engine had a sort of reprieve with the 166MM Series II, a Sports racing car that was almost entirely reserved for private stables, and when the 250MMs were put to the same use for three-liter engines, the factory experimented with several Sports racing cars with four-cylinder engines derived from the two-liter engine of the single-seater 1952 and 1953 world champion.

In 1954, two four-cylinder Sports racing cars derived from these prototypes, the two-liter 500 Mondial and the three-liter 750 Monza, took the place of the twelve-cylinder cars in the catalog. This move was a reasonable success; in two years, no less than thirty-five Mondials and forty Monzas left Maranello. In 1956, when the 250GT was establishing itself, the four-cylinder, three-liter engine was abandoned and only one Sports racing car

remained in the catalog, the 500 Testa Rossa. Nevertheless, the chassis evolved more than the four-cylinder engine, and it was the same for the 500TRC which followed a year later.

The work of the Maranello technical team—which had been remodeled following Lancia's handing over of power and Lampredi's departure—was only embryonic on the Ferraris of 1956. It developed fully in 1957. This maturing was reflected in the 500TRC; its low contours suggest a considerably modernized chassis. The advanced TRC cast the 500TR's looks as a dinosaur.

For its final year of service, the four-cylinder engine created by Lampredi in 1951 was considerably modified. Still present, of course, was the principle of the cylinder/cylinder-head block, two overhead camshafts driven by a series of gears arranged in front of the block and the double ignition by two distributors driven from the front of the crankshaft. The engine, Tipo 136C, kept the 90 mm bore and the 78 mm stroke of the 1952 500F2, but the top end was redesigned to reduce its height. The compression ratio for the 500TRC went from 8.5:1 to 8.75:1 and with the same twin horizontal Weber 40 DCO carburetors, the maximum strength of the engine was 190

It makes its precursor look like a dinosaur

horsepower at 7500 rpm compared to 180 at 7000 rpm for the 500TR.

Since 1956, the axle-mounted gearbox on the 500TR had been replaced by a four-speed gearbox coupled to the engine and the de Dion axle by a rigid axle-tree. By reworking the design of the space frame chassis and installing the squatter 136C engine in it, Massimino allowed Scaglietti to create a sleeker body, similar to the first of the contemporary four-cam vehicles. The profile was less rectilinear, with four pronounced bulges above the wheels and an indented front wheel housing design.

Red for aesthetic detail, yellow in memory of victory

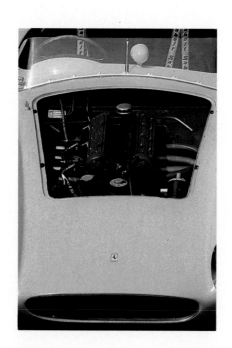

The low mouth at the front resulted in a low hood, which was in turn longer and more plunging. Finally, there were adjustments to comply with the new regulations laid down in annex "C" of the International Sporting Code, hence the name 500TRC. The rules applied to, among other things, the passenger door on the left, the small vehicle top device and the apron which protected both the driver and the passenger.

Ferrari devoted the 1957 Sports racing championship to the four-cam and the development of the future three-liter Testa Rossa. The 500TRC could thus play its role as the customer Sports racing car to the full; it also served as a basis, at least as far as the chassis was concerned, for the development of the 250 Testa Rossa which replaced it in 1958. About twenty 500TRCs were sold throughout the world.

The 500TRC was not only attractive, it also proved to be effective, particularly in the events of the 1957 world championship where it repeatedly made its mark in the two-liter category. At the Le Mans twenty-four-hour race, for example, victory in the two-liter class fell to Bianchi and Harris, with an average speed of 161.212 km/h in a yellow-and-green 500TRC from the Belgian national team.

We cannot reproach Daniel Heuberger for choosing this Belgian yellow—which also represents the color of Modena in the Ferrari insignia—when he restored his 500TRC.

Power, beauty, success

If the Mas du Clos collection is the finest in the world, it is not due solely to its completeness, but also because rarely does more than half an hour pass between the moment a chosen Ferrari leaves the museum and the moment it roars off along the ribbon of asphalt winding through the hills of the Massif Central. In the garage beside the track, Pierre Bardinon, the master of the house, selects a crash helmet from the period of the car in question and watches the care being lavished by Paul Coste and Bernard Lecour: filling up with fuel and oil, checking the tire pressures and starting up.

Today, Bardinon settles behind a Nardi four-arm steering wheel, which has been held in turn by Peter Collins, Maurice Trintignant, Wolfgang von Trips, Mike Hawthorn and Luigi Musso. The two British aces in fact had more confidence in these four aluminum arms surrounded by wood than in the usual steering wheel with three frail spokes. Does this mean that handling the 335 Sport is not child's play? Bardinon does not deny it, but he also acknowledges that the finest front-engined Ferrari Sports racing cars are the four-cam cars made for the 1957 world Sports racing championship. Wine being Bardinon's second passion, he knows that 1957 was an exceptional cru at Ferrari and he long ago chose this 335 Sport to represent that first-class vintage in his collection of racing Ferraris.

To counter the colossal 450S of their Maserati neighbors, the Maranello team played the trump they had acquired from the Lancia legacy. As a result, Scuderia Ferrari's 1957 monsters wrote several unforgettable pages of racing history. The premier racing four-cam Ferraris made an impact at the legendary Mille Miglia. They were the first cars to surmount a 200 km/h per lap average at Le Mans. They also brought Maranello a fourth world

Another product of 1957, a great vintage year: the 335 Sport, only four of which survive today. The most beautiful, 0674, is at Mas du Clos.

Mike Hawthorn and Peter
Collins preferred the more
robust four-spoke steering
wheel.

On the following page:
Luigi Musso, Maurice
Trintignant, Peter Collins
and 0674 at Sebring.

Wolfgang von Trips and
0674 at the Mille Miglia.

Car 0674 at the start of the
Le Mans twenty-four-hour
race.

title by toppling Maserati's reign. Power, beauty and success.

Following the 1956 Swedish Grand Prix double which gave Ferrari its third world championship, the new Maranello team set to work to prepare for 1957, its second season. The first stage was to adapt cylinder heads—each with two camshafts—to the V-12 Tipo 130 block of the 290MMs. The twelve-cylinder block in a sixty-degree V-shape was not radically modified; it kept its dimensions and its 3490 cc capacity. Yet the top end, which had been designed with this in mind, was reshaped to accommodate the four overhead camshafts. Had not one of the treasures inherited from Lancia been the Formula 1 V-8? On the Ferrari V-12, four camshafts—driven by triplex chains—now directly operated the large valves (35 mm for the inlet and 29 mm for the exhaust) by means of mushroom-headed tappets with twin concentric helical springs. By abandoning pin springs, space was found for the twenty-four spark plugs, two per cylinder. The plugs were screwed into the middle of the two sixty-degree Vees which formed the inlet

and exhaust valves. The four six-point distributors were also replaced by two twelve-point devices driven off the rear of the inlet camshafts. Several types of carburetor were planned, six twin 42 DCN Webers or three quadruple C 40P IIs, in particular. The engine produced 350 horsepower at 7200 rpm. This first four-cam engine was called the Tipo 136 for the 290 Sport and was followed by the Tipo 140 for the 315 Sport which, re-bored to 76 mm, brought the capacity to 3783 cc and the horsepower to about 360 with the engine running at slightly less than 7800 rpm. Finally, the Tipo 141 for the 335 Sport appeared with about 390 horsepower and a capacity increased to 4023 cc due to a new bore and a new track rod assembly.

Five chassis were made to any one of the these three engines. The multitubular chassis, called 520Bs, were a logical development of the 520s of 1956. Consequently, many features of the latter were still to be found: the 2350 mm wheelbase, the wishbones and helical springs at the front, the de Dion axle at the rear, the four-speed axle-mounted gearbox

The trump cards held by an heiress

In the face of formidable competition, the 335S found its place in the most prestigious records of automobile racing history.

and the enormous, well-ventilated drum brakes—the magnificent survivors of a condemned technique.

The structure was lowered to improve the main cross-section, and Scaglietti covered the five chassis with bodies that were successively more curved than those of 1956. The results were both aggressive and sumptuous. Subtle details differ between the five treasures, distinguishing each one and reflecting on the development of Scaglietti's art. Thus, 0646 (or 676?) and 0656, which made an unsuccessful appearance at Buenos Aires, with the 3.5 liter engine, were recognized by the rounded upper lip of their radiator grilles and their accentuated rear wings. Car 0674, which made its debut at Sebring with the 3.8 liter engine, also had pronounced rear wings, but its wide radiator grille gave it a still more feline appearance; this is the Mas du Clos car pictured here. Cars 0684 and 0700 entered the Mille Miglia with oval radiator grilles and rear wings that blended into rounded tails.

A quick survey of the 1957 season is enough to give an idea of the various roles the five cars played. At Sebring, Collins and Trintignant, who had been assigned to 0674, only came in sixth, having had repeated tire and brake problems. In the Mille Miglia, von Trips drove 0674, which was still equipped with the 3.8 liter engine. He finished second, just behind winning car 0684, driven by Piero Taruffi.

Wrapped up in legalities following Alfonso de Portago's tragic accident, 0674 and 0684 were absent from the Nurburgring, where 0656 and 0700 were helpless against Tony Brooks' Aston Martin with its disc brakes.

At Le Mans, Collins and von Trips piloted 0700, Hawthorn and Musso 0674, while Stuart Lewis-Evans and Martino Severi had been called in as reinforcements to replace Portago in 0684. The latter was the sole car to make the finish: Collins withdrew in the second lap, followed by Hawthorn shortly afterward. Before the 4.1 liter 0674 gave up, Hawthorn had

Four camshafts, six carburetors and 390 horsepower, requiring great skill and strength.

nevertheless established a lap record of 3 minutes 59.6 seconds or 203 km/h. The 200 km/h barrier had been broken for the first time and the record was to hold for four years.

At the Swedish Grand Prix at Kristianstadt, the positions in the world championship logically made Scuderia Ferrari play safe. Moss and Jean Behra's 450S Maserati came in first ahead of Collins and Hill in 0700. Hawthorn and Musso took fourth place in 0674.

The two cars appeared again at Caracas for the last round, which earned the world championship for Ferrari. Four Ferraris took the top four positions: Collins and Hill in 0700, followed by Hawthorn and Musso in 0674 once more. The two 250 Testa Rossa prototypes completed the quartet, providing a preview of the season to come. With the limiting of engine capacities, things would never be the same again.

TR for triumphant and red

The two TR58 prototypes at the 1957 Swedish Grand Prix.

Luigi Musso and 0728 at the Targa Florio.

Car 0728 before Gendebien and Hill's win at the Le Mans twenty-four-hour race.

For several seasons, events open to Sports racing cars brought a deliberate escalation of engine capacity, horsepower and thus speed. The 1958 ruling of the Commission Sportive Internationale reduced the engine capacity of cars admitted to the manufacturers' world championship to three liters. Ferrari envisaged at least three ways of conforming to these new requirements. A three-liter version of the four-cam V-12 would have been too heavy; adapting the new Formula 1, 2.5 liter V-6 engine required much more work. On the other hand, the success of the 250GT Competition berlinettas in the Gran Turismo category had underlined the possibilities of the three-liter two-cam V-12 engine. This was the solution chosen. Engineer Andrea Fraschetti inclined toward the three-liter V-12, originally called the Colombo, and the 1957 season was put to good account by experimenting on two prototypes and the large four-camshaft engines.

The first prototype of the three-liter Sports racing Ferrari, 0666, appeared discreetly on May 26, 1957, at the Nurburgring 1,000 Kilometer race. The second, 0704, made its debut at Le Mans, one month later, with its front wings detached to provide better ventilation for the brake drums, a practice which did not go unnoticed. Experiments on the two cars continued at the two last rounds of the 1957 championship in Sweden on August 11 and in Venezuela on November 3.

The 2953 cc Sports racing model is therefore derived from the great 250GT. The dimensions are identical but the team—revived by the Lancia heritage—made several modifications. The large elliptical springs were retained,

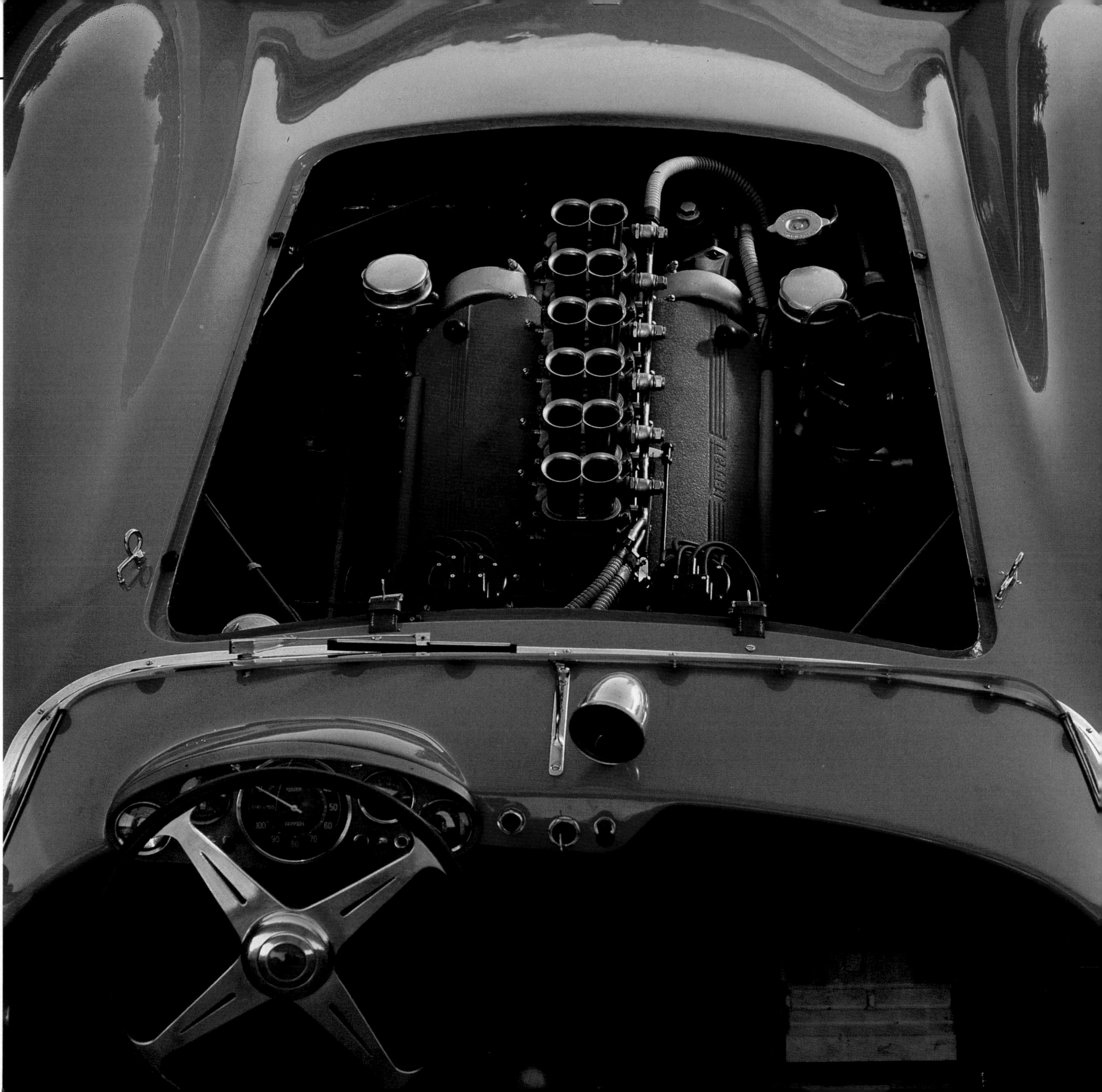

unlike in the 130, 140 and 141, which had gone over to helical springs. Relocating the twelve spark plugs outside the Vee to between the exhaust ports, provided the necessary space to reinforce the cylinder heads' attachment to the block, allowing the compression ratio to be increased without resorting to fixed cylinder heads. The space created between the banks of cylinders also allowed ventilation to be improved. Six 38 mm twin Weber carburetors supplied the hemispherical combustion chambers via individual pipes carefully coordinated with the exhaust manifolds. The dimensions of the valves—two per cylinder—were increased. Finally, following the example of the Formula 1 engines, the track rods were no longer forged but were manufactured from a block of steel for optimum reliability at speed. The lubrication system used in the 250GT block, with wet sump and gear pump, was provisionally retained, but the horsepower output was increased to 300 at 7200 rpm. The chassis bore an identical 2350 mm wheelbase to that of the four-cam, yet it was derived from the chassis created for the 500TRC. The modernized chassis designed by Massimino was evident in the reduced weight, height and general dimensions of the car.

At a press conference on November 22, Ferrari unveiled the three-liter 250 Testa Rossa Sports racing model that was to replace the 500TRC. This was the customer version, nineteen of which would be sold to private stables. Still, the four TR 58s that the competition department reserved for the drivers of the Scuderia were to be quite different. They took the opposition by surprise.

Cars 0666 and 0704, the two prototypes from the previous season which were made on different, right-hand-drive chassis, reappeared at the first round at Buenos Aires with the new engine and indented front wings. They had kept the four-speed gearbox and the rigid axle-tree.

Cars 0726 and 0728, two new factory vehicles, were not ready before Sebring. They had the same standard body and left-hand drive but, due to a de Dion rear axle and a gearbox coupled to the differential, they behaved quite differently.

These four official 1958 250 Testa Rossas, being the most special, are of course also the most valuable today. The first, 0666 went into well-earned retirement in the United States after three accidents, which caused it to have three successive bodies. The second, 0704, is neighbors with a Bugatti Royale at the Dearborn Ford Museum. The third, 0726, is said to be in Brazil after having served as first prototype for the Testa Rossa 59. The fourth and last, 0728, the one in our photographs, joined the Mas du Clos collection in 1982 with a claim to fame that predestined it to return to France. This is explained by its story.

After the double win achieved by Hill/Collins in 0704 and Hawthorn/von Trips in 0666 at Buenos Aires, 0728 unsuccessfully entered its first race at Sebring with Hawthorn and von Trips, while 0704 renewed the achievement with Hill and Collins, in front of Musso and Gendebien's 0726. At the Targa Florio, Hawthorn and von Trips finished third in 0728 behind Musso/Gendebien in 0726 and a Porsche. At the Nurburgring, Moss' Aston Martin beat out Hawthorn/Collins in 0704. Wolfgang Seidel and Gino Munaron were fifth in 0728.

The Scuderia TRs appeared in Germany with streamlined bodies, the indented wings having been abandoned. They arrived at Le Mans in this new form, which was more aerodynamic and distinguished them quite obviously from the seven private 250 Testa Rossas present.

Never had victory at Le Mans been so coveted, and three manufacturers vied for the favors of the tipsters: Jaguar, five times winner; Aston Martin, twice second; and Ferrari, four times world champion—but not having won at Le Mans since 1954. In an almost constant downpour, the Testa Rossas overcame the handicap of their drum brakes, and Ferrari won back victory at Le Mans, thanks to Phil Hill, Olivier Gendebien and 0728.

In its place among Pierre Bardinon's collection, this historic Testa Rossa has returned to the land of its achievement.

Races and colors

When the idea of national racing colors was born at the beginning of the century, the recognized automobile clubs conferred so that each could choose a distinctive color. Thus the famous blue was assigned to France and green to England; red was initially given to the United States. The Automobile-Club d'Italia only adopted racing colors at a later stage, and chose a dark red hue, leading the Americans to swap their red for blue and white—white for the body and blue for the chassis. Obviously something else had to be thought of when the traditional side frames disappeared under the body. Legend attributes Briggs Cunningham with the idea of painting two longitudinal stripes along the body, to represent the two chassis side frames that had become invisible. The Cunninghams wore the new American uniform for the first time at Le Mans in 1951.

J. Edward Hugus, an American from Pittsburgh, Pennsylvania, patriotically painted this same decoration on the 250 Testa Rossa that was delivered to him just before the Sebring twelve-hour race. The luck of the colors did not hold true in Florida as the car suffered a broken valve spring, yet still managed to glide to an honorable eighth place. In the downpour at Le Mans three months later, Hugus and teammate Ernie Eriksson took turns at the wheel of *Lucybelle II* and passed the last post in seventh position.

Beneath this boat-like name painted on the right side—and also perfectly adapted to the 1958 version of the Sarthe race-cruise—one of the nineteen 250 Testa Rossas, built and sold in 1958, was hidden. Unlike the four vehicles used that season by the factory team, these customer Testa Rossas all had aluminum bodies indented at the front, produced uniformly by Scaglietti. Their lightened chassis, made of tubes welded around two robust side frames, were similar to those of the factory Testa Rossas, but a bit less refined, with a rigid rear axle and two longitudinal leaf springs. Nevertheless, this enabled them to offer racing

A "red head" in the American colors.

97

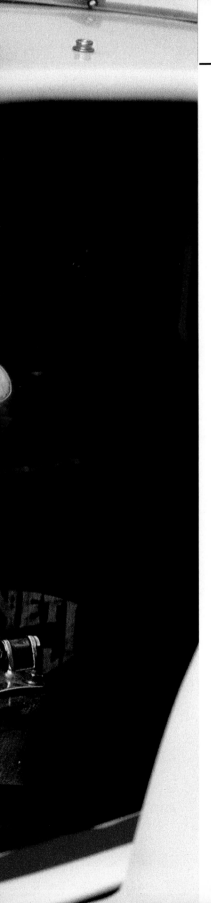

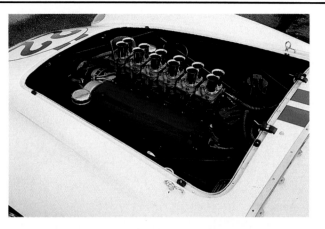

customers simpler maintenance and less arduous upkeep than that required by the de Dion axle. The left-hand-drive steering wheel was standard and no one managed—or asked—to have it otherwise. The single-camshaft three-liter V-12 engine, on the other hand, was common to both types of car, apart from details of fuel supply and exhaust. During the season, various trials with Solex carburetors and new exhausts were carried out on the factory Testa Rossas. The nineteen others invariably kept to the six twin Webers and to the exhaust system with two six-into-one manifolds connected to a pipe which was doubled under the doors ending up with four megaphones at the rear. With a compression ratio of 9.8:1, the new customer Sports racing Ferrari put out 300 horsepower at 7200 rpm. With a dry weight close to 1,700 lb. which represented considerable progress, the new 250 Testa Rossa compared well with the 190 horsepower of its equivalent in the previous year, the 500TRC.

Though more expensive than the TRC, the 250 Testa Rossa was sold only in slightly fewer numbers than its predecessor—nineteen vehicles compared with twenty-one. At a unit price of $11,800, equal to a Cadillac Eldorado Brougham, the United States took seven

The factory held onto four special Testa Rossas for itself; nineteen "standard" cars were sold, including 0732.

Drum brakes exposed before disappearing

with a hook to tow the beautiful Testa Rossa, which had been repainted dark blue, on a trailer. Bob Bodin discovered this Testa Rossa a few years ago and has set about restoring it to its past splendor.

The fascination of the 250 Testa Rossa— today moreso than ever—no doubt tends to make us forget the two congenital weaknesses of these superb machines. The first of these was the weight of their V-12 engines which made them understeer somewhat, a characteristic that was particularly noticeable on the customer cars because of their four-speed gearbox placed behind the engine. The gearbox on the factory versions was mounted on the axle with obvious reason and to a large extent compensated for the understeering faults. The second weakness, however, was common to all Testa Rossa twelve-cylinder vehicles. The drum brakes were inadequate despite their generous size and the extensive efforts made to cool them. Ferraris were not alone in having stayed faithful to drums. Porsche, for example, bore the same allegiance and only converted to discs in 1964 with the 904GTS. British competitors, Jaguar and Aston Martin in particular, had for years been singing the praises of disc brakes, but the discs were not sufficient to beat Ferrari in 1958.

250TRs; Venezuela, Brazil and Belgium two each; and the six others went to Finland, Switzerland, Italy, Austria, France and Cuba. Of the sixteen surviving today, one has remained in Brazil, one has gone to England, one is in France, two in Italy and eleven are to be found in the United States, including 0732, which was bought from Ed Hugus in 1959 by an eccentric amateur to enter in regional races. This amateur arrived at the races behind the wheel of a 250GT Tour de France equipped

Lucybelle II *before the deluge at the 1958 Le Mans twenty-four-hour race.*

One, two, three for a failed attempt

A new gearbox compensates for the moving of the engine to the left of the center.

The TR 59 may be immediately identified by its body. The design was more classic than that of the 1958 customer version, and may once again be credited to Pinin Farina. Nevertheless, it was brought into being by a new tradesman, Medardo Fantuzzi, a Modena craftsman who had hitherto devoted his talents exclusively to Maserati racers. Fantuzzi's small workshop was now charged with making the bodies for the Sports racing and single-seater Ferraris, while Scaglietti expanded from being a cottage industry to concentrate on the high-volume production of 250GT berlinettas and spyders. Pinin Farina, in its new Grugliasco factory, concerned itself with the manufacture of more luxurious private cars.

chanically as well. The traditional pin springs for the valves were replaced by helical springs. This technique, which ensured better operation at all speeds, also allowed the cylinder heads' attachment to the block to be reinforced. On the TR 59, these readjustments raised the horsepower of the three-liter V-12, now called 128/LM/59, to 308 at 7400 rpm.

This was combined with a reduction in weight obtained by resorting to different casings made from magnesium alloys, instead of the classic aluminum.

More important was the position of this engine in the Tipo 532 chassis, which retained the 2350 mm wheelbase and the de Dion axle. The engine was set off-center of the chassis by about 100 mm to the left. This was necessitated by a new five-speed gearbox, once again coupled to the engine, but in which only the secondary shaft was aligned with the new self-locking differential. Shifting the engine to the left made right-hand drive common on the TR 59.

The most important innovation concerned the brakes; the drums finally gave way to discs. After various trials, Ferrari had opted for the Dunlop system. The British firm also became Maranello's supplier of tires, after the Belgian factory owner, Englebert. The change to disc brakes also lightened the Ferraris by a further 55 lb. In all, the TR 59 had lost a total of more than 165 lb. while gaining in strength and braking power. Its main adversary would be

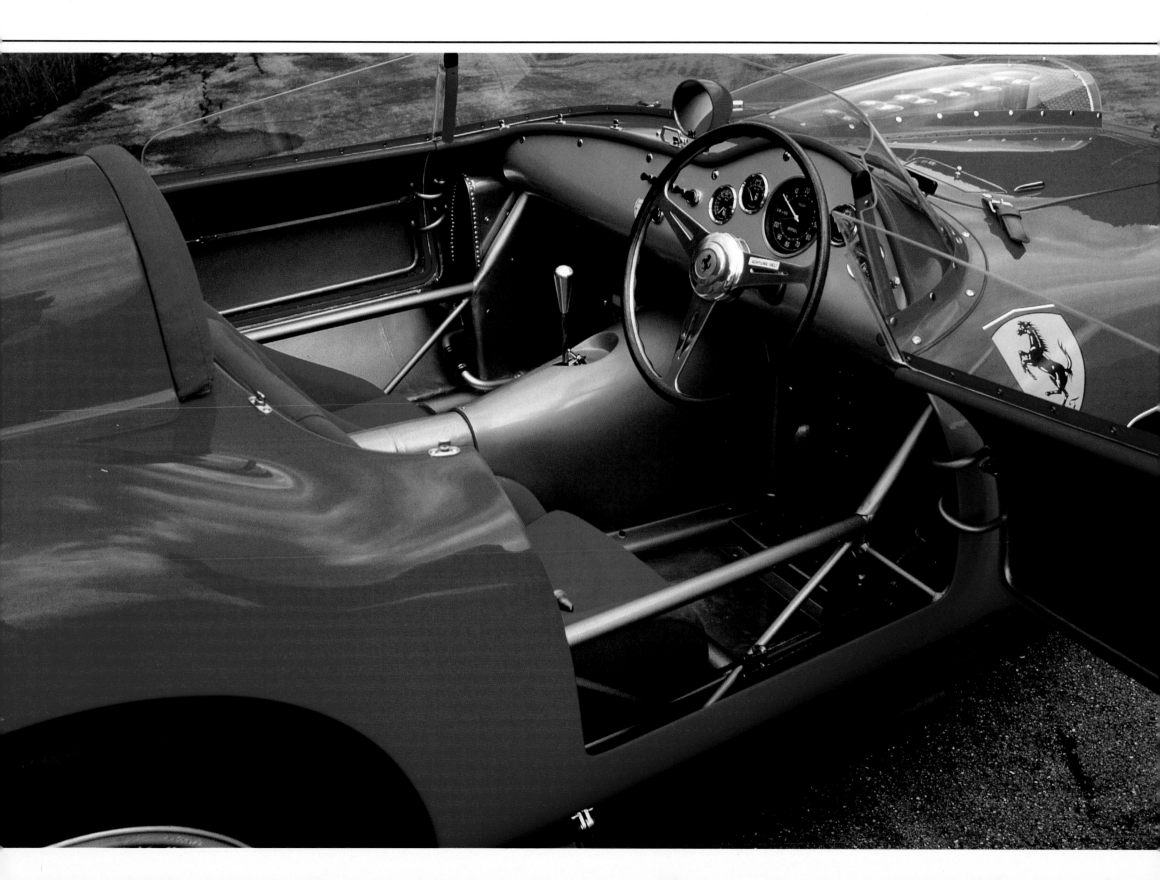

Car 0766 at the 1959 Le Mans twenty-four-hour race, at the Tourist Trophy and at Le Mans in 1960 (number 17).

the Aston Martin three-liter DBR1, which until then had been less powerful but rather more agile.

The TR 59 was reserved for Scuderia Ferrari and three vehicles were ready for the first round of the 1959 championship at Sebring: 0766, 0768 and 0770, the first being the car photographed here, owned by Albert Obrist. This first TR 59 boasts an epic career.

The victory won by 0766 at Sebring, first in the hands of Dan Gurney/Chuck Daigh, then Hill/Gendebien, was followed by the withdrawal of the three Testa Rossas at the Targa Florio. Stirling Moss triumphed at the Nurburgring with the sole Aston Martin entered; Hill/Gendebien were second in 0766 and Behra/Brooks third in 0768.

Meanwhile, two new TR 59s had come into being: 0772 and 0774. The second made its thundering debut in the hands of Behra by recording the best time at the Le Mans practice. Nevertheless, the twenty-four-hour race was a catastrophe for the three red cars: transmission problems for Cliff Allison and da Silva-Ramos in 0770 and engine problems for Behra and Gurney in 0774. Hill and Gendebien withdrew for the same reason, five hours before the finish, while in the lead with 0766.

The engine failure that deprived Ferrari of a fourth victory at Le Mans persuaded them to convert to dry-sump lubrication. The three Testa Rossas entered the last championship event, the Tourist Trophy in England. A sixth world title escaped Ferrari for reasons quite different from those that cost them Le Mans. Hill worked 0774's engine too hard in the first lap; Gurney lost precious time at the beginning of the race. Finally, a misunderstanding between the pits and Tony Brooks in 0766 deprived the Scuderia of second place—which would have limited its losses as Ferrari and Aston Martin would have tied for points. The 1959 championship cup went to Aston Martin and Ferrari had to make do with second place, still ahead of Porsche.

For 1960, two new Testa Rossas were built that differed again—although this fact was disguised by Fantuzzi's work—while 0770, 0772 and 0774 were reconstructed to the new specifications. Like its twin 0768, 0766 was sold. With the young Mexican brothers, Pedro and Ricardo Rodriguez, it had a fine run on the North American continent. It returned to Le Mans in 1960 and contributed to Ferrari's seventh world title by taking second. This second-place finish helped erase the insult of 1959 where, with a Ferrari first, second and third, 0766 was the best out of the unlucky TR 59s.

In 1957, the style of the 250GT berlinetta was transferred to the California, the prototype of which is shown here.

At the end of the 1962, Princess Saddrudin Aga Khan, the daughter-in-law of a well-off spiritual leader, put in an order to Geneva for a California Ferrari. The princess had good taste, and she will be forgiven for not knowing that the "California" that was delivered to her on February 1, 1963 (in a color she did not like), was a thoroughbred from a breed near extinction.

Today, this desirable Ferrari is called the short-wheelbase California. This is a familiar term for one of the rare Ferraris that has been given a real name: 250GT Spyder California. This official name, however, did not explain the full story.

The Spyder California had side windows, which could be closed by a few turns of a handle in bad weather, and an available hardtop, although it could not be carried in the car unless fixed in place. Yet even in the etymological sense of the term spyder, the Spyder California is actually a comfortable cabriolet—even if the top is not always easy to operate. The name "California"—an allusion to the land where the sky is reliable—was no doubt used as a reinforcement to remedy the approximation of the vocabulary.

The creator of these convertible 250GTs is attributed to Luigi Chinetti, as that of the Mercedes Benz 300SL roadsters is attributed to Max Hoffman. Chance dictated that these two people, both solid products of the Old World, should control the American dream car mar-

A princess' dream

ket from the vantage point of New York with its seasonal rigors.

Yet to understand the origin of these Californias, we must first turn to the 250GT berlinetta that is called the Tour de France today. Launched in 1955 for racing, the body of this wonderful berlinetta was first designed and fitted in various forms by Pinin Farina and later, from 1956 on, almost exclusively by Scaglietti. These berlinettas evolved continuously until 1964 and acquired an ever-growing share of the Gran Turismo category of the most famous races, the Tour de France among them.

In the spring of 1957, Scaglietti changed the design of the aluminum body that protected the chassis' 2600 mm wheelbase and the three-liter, 240 horsepower, V-12 engine. The first item noticed was that the headlights had been set back and streamlined into the wings, and that the upper edge of the rear wings was now horizontal. It is at this stage that the shape of the California spyder began; its prototype was finished in the last days of 1957.

Although they were not intended for competition, the first Californias were nothing more nor less than convertible berlinettas, both in appearance and construction, inside and out. Their bodies were made by Scaglietti and this distinguished them from the elegant 250GT cabriolets made in Pinin Farina's factory.

The berlinettas evolved above all with increased performance, which did not correspond directly to the vocation of the Californias, even though some people did not hesitate to take their beautiful convertibles out on the circuit. The Californias nevertheless benefited from several of these advances: new cylinder heads, new chassis, telescopic shock absorbers and disc brakes, in particular.

To begin with, disc brakes combined with a servo brake appeared as a replacement for the valiant drums. This took place in the autumn of 1959 at the same time as the short-wheelbase berlinetta was being presented at the Paris Salon. The chassis was termed short because the wheelbase was reduced from 2600 to 2400 mm—but it also differed in other ways.

Following the berlinetta, the Californias inherited an important modification to the engine. The pin springs on the valves were replaced by helical springs and the spark plugs were moved outside of the Vee, from the induction to the exhaust.

This important modification coincided with the adoption of telescopic shock absorbers,

The California—a convertible berlinetta

usually Koni. This was the end of the valiant Houdaille shock absorbers with arms, the winged drum brakes and the pin springs for the valves, which had all been habitually used in Ferraris since the end of the forties. The chassis from the new berlinetta was adapted to the California at the beginning of 1960; the first "short" California spyder, 1795 GT, was ready in March 1960.

As to the aesthetics, on the other hand, the changes were minor compared with the completely new design that Pinin Farina had given to Scaglietti for the berlinetta. Indeed, a close examination of the details is required to distinguish the new short-wheelbase Spyder California from the previous long-wheelbase one. For example, the air intake on the hood is embedded into it where it once protruded. It is also apparent that the top of the radiator grille is more open. The Borrani wheel rims had gone from sixteen inches to fifteen, and the exterior door handles were no longer flush, but protruding.

Yet more importantly than these details, the general balance had changed. The short-wheelbase spyder had lost 450 mm. It seemed to be squatter, less streamlined and more

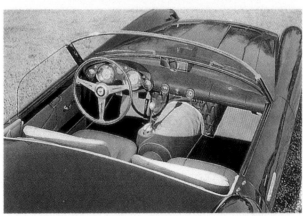

One of the last long-wheelbase Californias (1451 GT) before the 1959 Le Mans race.

A hardtop could always replace the convertible top, as here on 1795 GT.

aggressive, and this was reflected in its behavior. The new cylinder heads alone brought an additional forty horsepower. On paper, the power of the three-liter V-12 had increased from 240 to 280 horsepower. Whether or not this was optimistic, the short-wheelbase California was another Ferrari, both in the way it held the road and in its braking. This enhanced its performance at least as much as the additional horsepower with which it was credited.

From March 1960 to February 1963, fifty short-wheelbase Californias left the Maranello workshops. Apart from the running technical developments during the course of production and the incessant variations in detail from one car to another, numerous special requests were made. Sometimes the headlights were to be uncovered. Sometimes, although rarely, the ventilation inlets in the engine compartment were to be removed. Not to mention the various colors, of course. It is to be noted that red was not always a common choice in this period. Many options were permitted, but no one ever asked for—or received—a right-hand-drive car.

The most special short-wheelbase California is chassis number 2015 GT. It was finished just in time for Le Mans 1960, and was distinguished by its cylinder heads, camshafts and valves of the Testa Rossa type, its lightened track rods, a special exhaust, an extra-long axle and, accessible by means of a filler neck flush with the trunk, a fuel tank containing 120 liters instead of the usual 100. Bill Sturgiss,

Californian Ferrari in France

its American owner, and French hopeful, Jo Schlesser, brought it into eleventh place when the powerful V-12 engine—which probably approached 280 horsepower—decided otherwise, less than four hours from the finish. In the Gran Turismo category, however, it nevertheless had the three 250GT berlinettas and a Chevrolet Corvette in front of it.

Although derived from the berlinetta, the California was not intended for racing. The green car shown in these pages has had a peaceful existence; its four owners have only driven it 45,000 kilometers. The most serious difficulty it seems to have faced was when it was delivered. Sergio Scaglietti's green paint was not fortunate enough to please the princess who immediately ordered a "Jaguar" metallic green. This was immediately carried out at Henri Chapron's coachworks.

Car 3095 GT is among the five last Californias made. The last, 4137 GT, was delivered in February 1963. The name, California, was used again in 1966, but the spyder—a perfect combination of the three-liter V-12 engine, Scaglietti's skill and the sun of California—has remained without descendants.

Pininfarina: new name, new look

From the aerodynamic coupe at the top to the Superfast Series II at the bottom. In the middle, Sergio Pininfarina, Renzo Carli and the wooden buck of the 400SA. The finished car will be different, particularly at the front.

The 400 Superamerica made its first public appearance at the Brussels Salon in January 1960, but this new Ferrari was not a cabriolet and was not greatly noticed. The 400 Superamerica's design had in fact already been seen on the 250GT cabriolet presented at the Paris Salon a few months earlier, and its shortened chassis was not likely to improve its banal looks.

Although Pininfarina did not provide great stylistic innovation, the 400 that succeeded the 410 contained great technical advances, making up for the ground that the 410 had lost to the 250GT. The first consequence of the arrival of the 400 Superamerica was the disappearance of the large 4.9 liter V-12 Tipo 126A with fixed cylinder heads, the last descendant from the engine designed in 1950 by Lampredi. The new four-liter V-12, Tipo 163, which replaced it, returned to the more compact dimensions and the detachable cylinder heads of the first Ferrari V-12, the 1.5 liter designed in 1946 by Colombo.

By keeping the original exterior dimensions on the twelve-cylinder, sixty-degree, V-shaped block, the Maranello technicians managed to bring the total capacity up to 3967 cc. Com-

pared to the 250GT's 2953 cc, the bore increased from 73 to 77 mm and, with a new crankshaft, the stroke went from 58.8 to 71 mm. The twelve-cylinder engine thus retained its over-square configuration—this was essential. It also incorporated the most recent advances of the three-liter engine: spark plugs relocated on the exhaust side and helical valve springs.

It was noticed that, for the first time in the history of production Ferrari cars, the designation 400 no longer reflected the cylinder capacity (330.62 cc) but about one tenth of the total capacity. Disconcerted by such a break with tradition, some thought that this figure represented the engine's horsepower. Horsepower was in fact, as stated in the catalog, 340 at 7000 rpm with a compression ratio of 8.81:1 and three Weber 42 DCN, or at times Solex, carburetors.

The gearbox for the engine was essentially similar to the four-speed of the 250GT, but an electrically controlled overdrive became an option and the multidisc clutch of the 410 gave way to a more straightforward Fichtel & Sachs single disc system.

Compared with that of the 410, the new

chassis also presented some notable advances inherited from the 250GT. Dunlop shock absorbers and disc brakes allowed fifteen-inch Borrani rims to be used instead of the previous sixteen-inch rims. Finally, this chassis, Tipo 538, was markedly shorter. With a wheelbase of about 2420 mm instead of the previous 2600, it approached that of the most recent 250GT berlinettas.

The 400 Superamerica had only ever been sold as a cabriolet, until November 1960 when Pininfarina presented the experimental coupe, Superfast II, at the Turin Salon. The second car of this name, following the experimental 410 unveiled in Paris five years earlier, this coupe with its totally novel style left no one indifferent. Its profile resembled the wing of an aircraft, with its penetrating leading edge, its progressively expanding shape providing the best possible airflow over its finely tapered trailing edge. The leading edge incorporated a discreet elliptical air inlet, decorated with an aluminum grille with rectangular holes—the only concession to Maranello tradition. The last drop of superfluity in the design was removed by the retractable headlights and the roof was just as successfully adapted to this wing-like profile. The slightly curved uprights, the slanted windshield and the elegance with which the roof dome blended into the rear were greatly admired. This pleasant form would be repeated, with all its dimensions retained, on the Porsche 911 a few years later.

These avant-garde forms were created in the new factory that Pininfarina (the firm's name was also in a new form, being written in one word) had just opened at Grugliasco on the edge of Turin. But for the moment, the cars remained experimental and this is no doubt why the Superfast II was not labeled a Superamerica and did not include all the elements of the 400 Superamerica. Despite its chassis number (2207 SA), which came from a much later date than the first cabriolet (1611 SA), the Superfast II was more of a compromise between the 410 and the 400. Thus, it shared with the new model the reduced 2420 mm

Enzo Ferrari ordered this metallic green coupe with leather and Peugeot cloth upholstery for himself.

117

Style outstripped method

wheelbase, the disc brakes and, in all probability, the four-liter engine. The classic Houdaille shock absorbers were still present.

This time, style preceded technology and the Superfast II, a study in bodywork with no declared outlet, was the star of the Turin Salon. It was seen again at the Brussels Salon in January 1961 with a few alterations. An air inlet had been made on the hood above the carburetors, discreet turn indicators adorned the front wings, deflectors on the doors improved the ventilation of the cockpit and the streamlining on the rear wheels had disappeared. Meanwhile, Pininfarina had received an order from Maranello, a justified homage to its achievements: a limited production of 400 Superamericas with bodies in the same style.

In fact, the design of the 400SA coupe only differed from that of the adapted Superfast II by its headlights. These were no longer retractable, but encased under plastic covers streamlined to the shape of the wings. Thirteen other orders followed the first one, thereby eclipsing the cabriolet which only owed its relative success—six of them were produced—to its earlier arrival. Therefore, between March 1961 and August 16, 1962, the date the last one was

delivered, fourteen 400SA coupes left Grugliasco, about one per month.

This limited production made it possible to cater to personalized orders: headlights that were or were not streamlined (which radically altered the front), flush or protruding door handles, possible streamlining on the rear wheel housings and so on. Venetian Count Giovanni Volpi thus obtained a black car (2809 SA) made from aluminum, with removable headrests, streamlined headlights and rear wheel housings. Prince Bernhard of the Netherlands set his heart on a green coupe with straight headlights but with a 250GT engine (2613 GT).

Pininfarina's coachwork even covered two 250GT Competition 61 cars, one of which served as the prototype to the 250GTO. While the GTO was following a different path, it did not prevent Enzo Ferrari from succumbing to the charm of the "coupe aerodinamico." Indeed, he ordered, for his own personal use, a green 400SA (3097 SA) with unstreamlined headlights and—a strange refinement—leather and beige cloth upholstery made by Peugeot. It is true that cloth is less slippery and more absorbent than leather, but the link that always existed between Sochaux, Grugliasco and Maranello should not be forgotten. This link was also reflected by the presence of a disconnectable Peugeot ventilator under the hood of the Superamerica.

John Lamm photographed this distinguished car in its retirement in California: it is still green, but has lost its cloth upholstery.

In the cockpit of 3097 SA, leather has now replaced cloth.

Aerodynamic
and trendy

While the production of the exclusive 400 Superamerica coupe aerodinamico continued at the craftsman's rate of about one vehicle per month, the Superfast II continued its evolution at Pininfarina. At the Geneva Salon in March 1962, the Superfast III was thus on display.

The Superfast III was an experimental and fascinating development of the coupe aerodinamico. The uprights on the side windows were reduced to thin pillars, thereby increasing the surface of glass to the maximum possible.

The most noticeable innovation, however, was at the front, where the radiator grille with its rectangular holes was replaced by an air inlet that was still elliptical but which could be closed. A pivoting panel hidden beneath the front could reduce the amount of air let in until the orifice was completely shut, forming a perfectly smooth, profiled nose. This mechanical device was controlled by a thermostat and the needle of a "calandra" dial installed on the extreme left of the dashboard, providing the driver with a continuous indication of the panel's position. A manual control was also provided. In addition, the hood was

once more completely smooth and the rear wheel housings were streamlined. This attention to profile produced a beautiful effect.

Constructed on the chassis of the Superfast II (2207 SA), this sumptuous exercise in style had an ephemeral existence, however. Only a few months after Geneva, the whole layout of its beautiful shape was disrupted by the addition of two protruding headlights and the return to a classic, elliptical radiator grille. The same chassis, 2207 SA, had thus become Superfast IV, a car which never was honored by show at a salon. Nevertheless, it still retained the panel-opening gauge on its dashboard, a useless reminder of its past splendor. In August 1962, 2207 SA was handed over to an industrialist from Milan, Nicolo de Nora, who had also just bought the manufacturing rights for the first "small" Ferrari, the ASA 1000.

Superfast IV is therefore the only one of the three Superfasts to have survived; it is also thus responsible for the disappearance of Superfast II and Superfast III.

It is also a matter for regret that Maranello was not convinced by Superfast III when it

Ferrari preferred an elongated wheelbase version of the superb Superfast III by Pininfarina. There was still a choice between faired and unfaired headlights.

An extra twenty centimeters for the Series II car

was decided to develop the coupe aerodinamico. The 400 Superamerica was progressing in a different direction, adopting the 2600 mm wheelbase of the 250GT 2+2 launched in 1960. This was certainly in response to a desire for standardization but also gave the remodeled coupe increased space inside without, however, providing it with two additional seats. The long wheelbase fortunately produced a less deplorable effect on the aesthetics of the coupe than on the cabriolet and it is necessary to look at the two coupes closely in order to notice a slight imbalance and to appreciate how easy it must be to destroy a perfect form, even by just lengthening it.

The wheel tracks also increased, going from 1359 to 1395 mm at the front and from 1350 to 1370 mm at the rear. On the other hand, performance declined somewhat, particularly due to the carburetors which had been reduced from 42 to 40 mm.

Deliveries of these exceptional Ferraris nevertheless continued at the same rate of one per month. The first Series II coupe aerodinamico (3931 SA) was introduced at the London Salon in October 1962. The eighteenth and last (5139 SA) was delivered in January 1964. During the same period, the 400 Super-

america long-wheelbase cabriolet found only four buyers.

This second series also generated fewer special orders. No different engines are known of and variations in the bodywork seem to have been limited to the option of streamlined rear wheel housings and the position of the headlights. The streamlined headlights, which are more pleasing but give less light, were more popular than the protruding ones, which always produced a less successful front.

There should therefore be a total of thirty-two surviving coupe aerodinamicos, not including the three Superfasts. This is fewer than the thirty-eight 250GTOs. In fact, about ten of the coupe aerodinamicos are missing, and few of them seem to have received the consideration (or restoration) due their rank. It is surprising that these super-Ferraris have thus remained in the shadow, although this discretion somehow suits their refinement. Even if there are Ferraris that are like good stories, the best is not necessarily the last— nor the longest.

Three elements, panoramic vision, wire grille covered headlights and radiator mesh for touring.

Ten years after

In 1950, Nuccio Bertone became a pioneer by acquiring a Ferrari 166 Mille Miglia, one of the Touring barchettas that were both attractive and efficient. The young body maker competed in several races and even in the 1950 Mille Miglia. At the Turin Salon in April 1950, Carrozzeria Bertone presented a small cabriolet with a two-liter Ferrari engine whose history has remained mysterious. This cabriolet disappeared soon after and no other Bertone Ferrari was seen for many long years. The creator of the unforgettable Alfa Romeo Giulietta Sprint went on to become the other great Italian body maker, but without ever touching another Ferrari.

An interval of ten years elapsed until in March 1960 at the Geneva Salon, a second Bertone Ferrari appeared. It bore the signature of a young Piedmontese designer.

Giorgetto Giugiaro was in fact only twenty-one when Bertone took him on to replace Franco Scaglione in December 1959. The Bertone Ferrari was the third of the twenty-one cars that Giugiaro designed at the carrozzeria before going on to Ghia and later his own carrozzeria, creating Ital Design in 1968.

The Bertone Ferrari coupe, which was fairly classic, although painted an original metallic light green color, was distinguished not only by the beauty of its shape and the care taken over its finish, but also by the radical reversal of the whole design philosophy that Pinin Farina had created for the short-wheelbase 250GT berlinetta.

Whereas Pinin Farina remained faithful to the two-compartment racing formula for its 250GT, Bertone presented a three-compartment design which at once promised quite different performance. The large area of glass obtained by the thin pillars provided panoramic visibility which was definitely more touristic than Pinin Farina's plexiglass rear window and opaque rear side panels. The spaciousness of the cockpit and the trunk left no doubt

Best possible access to the engine is provided by an integral hood-fender engine cover and the dashboard breaks new ground with its angled dials.

as to the intended use of the car. This was confirmed inside by the electric windows and the attractive dashboard which was no longer purely functional. The beautiful light alloy wheels, specially cast by Campagnolo, provided a modern alternative to the traditional spoke wheels of Borrani. The hood and front wings could be lifted up together toward the front to uncover the engine completely. The headlights, with their wire mesh covering, were more suited to driving down country lanes than to roaring around the asphalt of a race circuit.

Bertone's creation was intended for a completely different use but its foundations were identical to those of the new Scaglietti berlinetta, the most recent of the 250GTs offered by Ferrari to those of its customers interested in racing. Scaglietti's 250GT continued the quest for racetrack performance that presided over the development of the berlinetta, unveiled at the Paris Salon in October 1959. Thus the wheelbase of the chassis was reduced by 200 mm to increase driveability; the

An alternative to the typical racing berlinetta by Scaglietti, top, Bertone's study underwent a few minor alterations before being sold.

Giugiaro's first Ferrari was also his penultimate one

disc brakes made their first appearance on a Gran Turismo Ferrari; the friction-based shock absorbers had given way to tubular, telescopic ones; and the three-liter V-12 engine combined the latest progress inspired by racing on the 250GTs and the Testa Rossas. Initially, this short wheelbase berlinetta was only intended for racing—and this was the basis on which Bertone worked, since the chassis that he obtained was the fourth (1739 GT) in a series of about forty-five cars made between the end of 1959 and the end of the 1960 season.

What was Nuccio Bertone thinking of? He must have wanted to attract Ferrari's attention with a touring-car-type version of the 250GT berlinetta. In fact, the new berlinetta 250GT was a little outside his specialty. Whereas the long-chasis berlinettas were for racing, the new model, without abandoning any of its sporting pretensions, had a civilian version added to it, which looked identical.

Even if it was not totally without use, Bertone's move was of no benefit to his firm since

the Lusso berlinettas that Ferrari began to produce during 1960 were all covered by the body that Pinin Farina had designed for the racing version. Twenty cars were thus sold from June 1960 on with their power reduced by thirty horsepower and the weight increased by at least 220 lb. due solely to the material used—steel instead of aluminum. The price of luxury.

While the aluminum berlinettas were laying down the law on the racetracks and the Lussos were attracting a different clientele to Maranello, the beautiful Bertone coupe, condemned to remain a sole specimen, was sold to Sr. Wax, a Genoese industrialist and lover of special car bodies. In November, however, the white coupe with its green leather upholstery was put on show on the Bertone stand at the Turin Salon. A few changes were apparent: the stainless steel roof had returned to its natural color, Pirelli tires replaced the Continentals and, on the side, a discreet inscription, prototipo E.W., showed the initials of the new owner.

British, blue and brave

―――

In 1961, as if to celebrate its first birthday, the short-wheelbase 250GT berlinetta was diversified into three different models: the Lusso road version, with a steel body and an engine of about 230 horsepower; a "normal" racing version, with an aluminum body and an engine of about 270 horsepower; and a special racing version, also with an aluminum body but whose engine created more than 280 horsepower.

At the end of the 1960 racing season, Maranello added another strong dose of vitamins to the most powerful 250GT engine. The new engine had larger valves, reinforced helical valve springs working with camshafts with a higher lift (10 mm instead of 9) and reworked combustion chambers which brought the compression from 9.5:1 to 9.7:1. The fuel supply came via three Weber 46 mm carburetors, instead of the previous 40 mm ones, and redesigned inlet and exhaust manifolds opening into tuned exhausts. The engine, called 168 Comp. 61 in the local jargon, produced more than 280 horsepower; the 1960 racing version only reached 270 horsepower on rare occasions.

This redeployment of horsepower was, moreover, combined with a noticeable reduction in weight (even though this cannot be precisely quantified), obtained both in the engine, by the use of still lighter alloys for the block and some castings, and in the chassis and body.

The differences are subtle, but Pininfarina had modified their design in numerous points and, on the 1961 berlinettas, which were still produced at Scaglietti, there no longer existed any one piece of the body that was interchangeable with those of the previous year.

Of course, the 280 horsepower berlinetta was the most sought after by racing customers, but only twenty-two of them had their wish granted. Forty-six of the 1960 racing berlinettas had been produced.

This is where two legendary people appeared on the scene, Robert R. C. Walker and Stirling Moss. Walker was a gentleman of Scottish origin who had always owned the best

This berlinetta, the only right-hand-drive one and decorated in the colors of the Rob Walker Racing Team, holds the most race victories of all the twenty-two made.

After an accident, the berlinetta that Stirling Moss made famous had a new body built on it by Drogo at Modena.

cars and been able to attract the best drivers into his stable. The Rob Walker Racing Team cars traditionally sported a navy blue livery decorated with a transverse white stripe at the front. For several years, Walker had also held a trump in his game in the person of Moss, an all-time great. In 1960, Moss had already successfully driven Walker's first navy blue berlinetta. It was therefore not surprising to find him at the wheel of the latest berlinetta model in 1961. It is this car, 2735 GT, the only right-hand-drive one built, that is photographed here in its retirement in England—a peaceful retirement after a very eventful career.

Walker received 2735 GT at Le Mans in June 1961, just before the start of the greatest of the endurance races; the car was entered with Moss and Graham Hill sharing the wheel. The blue berlinetta, bearing the number 18, was in third place until a fan blade sheared, cutting through a radiator hose and causing the engine to overheat and break down. After being repaired at Modena, the car was at Silverstone on July 8, where Moss won the British Empire Trophy with it, beating the lap record.

At Brands Hatch, one month later, Moss gave a repeat performance. For the second year running, the Tourist Trophy was held as a four-hour event at Goodwood. Moss was faced by Mike Parkes, in another 250GT berlinetta, several Aston Martin DB4GTs and a pack of special E-type Jaguars. Moss won, his sixth Tourist Trophy. Parkes, who came in second, said about Moss: "I have learnt more about driving this afternoon than on any other occasion."

The exploits of Stirling Moss and 2735 GT came to a happy end in the Caribbean, in December, with their victory in the Nassau Tourist Trophy. Moss was by then almost a member of Scuderia Ferrari and took part notably in the development of the prototype GTO. Rob Walker sold the glorious blue berlinetta; in five races it had only lost once.

The following Tourist Trophy, once more held at Goodwood, was unhappy for 2735 GT, which then belonged to Christopher Kerrison. A bad crash meant that it had to be completely rebuilt. The operation was carried out at Modena, by Giorgio Neri and Luciano Bonancini for the mechanicals and Piero Drogo for the body. Like another 250GT bfore it, 2735 GT lost its famous color and was rebuilt into a pseudo GTO.

It was not until 1985 that Clive Beecham, the tenth owner, had the happy idea of returning the blue mantle to the car that was certainly the most outstanding of the twenty-two Competition 61 berlinettas.

Giorgetto and Cleopatra

Ⅰt would be a pity if Bertone's second 250GT passed into posterity due only to its nose. It was certainly a successful and indeed attractive nose, but it was not enough to make up for the rest of the car. It was more the overall perfect harmony of this car than its generous nostrils that made its success. The treatment of the nose was only ever an adaptation of the one invented for the Ferrari single-seater 156 F1, champion of the world in 1961, and for the Sports prototypes. The initiative was no doubt due to the engineer, Carlo Chiti, who that year had created a small-scale wind tunnel to take care of the aerodynamics of the Ferraris. By taking up this original detail, Giorgetto Giugiaro, the young Bertone designer, managed to integrate its curves into a body design that was novel in every way.

Carrozzeria Bertone revealed this interesting exercise at the Geneva Salon in March 1962. In 1960, exactly two years earlier, Bertone had unveiled on this same stand a first 250GT coupe which was just as original and was signed by the same stylist. The comparison between these two offerings, with a two-year interval between them, is not without interest; they are vastly different designs. From the stretched lines of his first 250GT to the compact roundness of the second, Giugiaro showed great eclecticism.

In 1960, Bertone had anticipated this tendency by proposing a deliberate touring version of the short-wheelbase 250GT berlinetta which had just been launched for racing. Even if the Turin bodyworker's proposition was not taken up in its original form by Ferrari, the idea nevertheless took root in the 250GT Lusso, an alternative to the racing berlinetta which became available soon after.

When Bertone made his second proposition, the context had changed. Whereas in 1960, the production of luxurious berlinettas was considerably smaller than that of the racing versions, from 1961 on, the Lusso berlinetta became increasingly successful. This may be explained by the fact that, despite their similar looks, due to the unchanging Pininfarina design executed by Scaglietti, the two types of berlinettas became more and more different. One became more sophisticated; the other

Its nose made it famous, but the second and last 250GT by the designer Giorgetto Giugiaro had other assets.

136

The 250GT Lusso presented at the 1961 Geneva Salon, a design by Pininfarina, was executed by Scaglietti.

Car 3269 GT before alterations.

Prince Bernard of the Netherlands obtained a coupe aerodinamico made by Pininfarina on the same base.

became more centered around racing. The divergence reached its zenith when the 250GTO arrived in 1962.

In 1961, all the 250GT berlinettas had adopted a new engine block to which the cylinder heads were attached by means of four bolts instead of three. Apart from this common characteristic, the road models differed from the racing models in many respects: camshafts with a smaller lift, 40 mm carburetors instead of 46 mm ones, smaller valves, heavier-duty track rods, untuned exhausts. Less-rounded pistons also gave a more urbane compression ratio, on the order of 9.2:1 instead of 9.4:1. This was reflected in the horsepower, however, which fell from more than 280 to about 230.

As in 1960, the 1961 Lusso differed from the racing version in the metal that Scaglietti used for the bodies as well. Steel replaced aluminum, providing a more polished appearance and a lower noise level in the passenger cell; the change also obviously had an effect on the

▮ An evocation of the world champion

weight. Several details of the exterior finish made it possible to recognize the Lusso: the fuel tank filler neck was hidden by a flap on the top of the rear left wing; a smaller-capacity fuel tank was chosen of ninety liters instead of 130 to provide more loading space in the trunk; and finally, the equipment in the cockpit was both more complete and more refined— leather upholstery, wind-up glass windows, cigar lighter and so on.

Added to the bulk of the body and the luxurious finish, the additional weight created by numerous components made of cast iron, instead of the ultralight Elektron metal used on the racing cars, including the gearbox casing, adding some 50 lb. to the Lusso. Despite their similar looks the Lusso behaved in a totally different—but above all, much easier—fashion than the racing 250GTs.

From the first presentation at the 1961 Geneva Salon until the start of 1963, about seventy-five Lussos were produced, only four of which were not covered with the standard Scaglietti body. Pininfarina dressed two as coupe aerodinamicos and one as a welded hardtop cabriolet. Nuccio Bertone was thus the only freelance bodyworker to be granted the favor of having a chassis (3269 GT). It is said that this dispensation was granted to him on the express condition that he not resell the car. Bertone did not in fact get rid of this superb two-seater immediately. He even found the time to change the color from its original

▌ Bertone, the only freelancer

navy blue to a becoming metallic gray, before it reappeared at the Turin Salon seven months later. A few alterations were made on this occasion; the Cavallino had been moved to the left-hand radiator grille and small inlets at the base of the rear side panel uprights aid ventilation of the cockpit.

Today, the two Bertone 250GTs are reunited under the same roof in Los Angeles, and Steve Tillack has restored them masterfully. If Bertone had to wait for ten more years to make the body for another Ferrari, was it because he was being made to pay for breaking his promise of selling this car?

Of the seventy-five Lusso models made in 1961 and 1962, three were given bodies by Pininfarina and only one by Bertone.

An "O" of surprise or admiration?

In 1962, the manufacturers' world championship was held for the Gran Turismo category for the first time. Giotto Bizzarrini, the engineer who had successfully led the development of the 250GT since its earliest years, was charged with increasing the car's range still further.

Bizzarrini saw that the short-wheelbase berlinetta had reached its limits. The cars had an over-large main cross-section, a front that offered too much wind resistance and a rear that was too narrow to accommodate tires that were growing relentlessly in width. Bizzarrini first tested a new body, a coupe aerodinamico specially made by Pininfarina from the design that for several months had been used for the small-scale production of the 400 Superamerica. The public first saw this experimental berlinetta (2643 GT) at Le Mans in June 1961. It was entered by Scuderia Ferrari with the local Fernand Tavano and Italy's great hope, Giancarlo Baghetti, as drivers.

Under the hood was a battery of six twin-choke Weber carburetors and a dry-sump engine with a separate oil tank. The berlinetta number 12 had to give up in the middle of the

Scaglietti translated into metal the shapes developed at Maranello.

Six carburetors and dry-sump lubrication inherited from the last Testa Rossas.

Giotto Bizzarrini, Stirling Moss and Willy Mairesse at Monza with the prototype that was to become the 250GTO.

night for mechanical reasons, and its stability at high speed had proved to be imperfect despite a rudimentary spoiler improvised at the rear. The attractive 2643 GT was thus left to one side and the development of the 250GT immediately took a different tack.

Of the two prototypes that followed, the first was tested at the Monza autodrome in early September 1961. Its provisional body, made at Maranello without any regard for aesthetics, contrasted strongly with Pininfarina's. But, despite its basic presentation, it foreshadowed the 1962 berlinetta on numerous points. Compared to the short berlinetta and the Pininfarina prototype, the air intake was greatly reduced, so much so that three triangular openings in the nose were made as reinforcement. In addition, two holes made on each side aided evacuation of the air admitted in the engine compartment and simultaneously facilitated the airflow.

The more steeply inclined windshield sheltered a lower cockpit and the back looked longer but also wider—to make room for the 700×15 tires—and squarer than that of the short-wheelbase berlinetta. There was one purpose behind the modifications: an improved main cross-section and a finer profile for increased performance.

The new berlinetta that was presented in the courtyard of the Maranello factory on February 24, 1962, was a synthesis of these exper-

■ Optimum 250GT

iments. Its red body, decorated with the Italian colors in a longitudinal band, was in fact nothing more than a "finished version" of the Monza prototype and, like it, came directly from the bodyshop in the factory.

The chassis, called 539/62 Comp., differed from that of the 1961 berlinetta allowing it to admit a slightly lower engine. It was this lowering of the engine that made possible the aerodynamic innovations.

Like the engine in the experimental Le Mans berlinetta, and before that, in the Testa Rossa barchettas, the three-liter V-12 engine had six twin-choke carburetors and was based on a dry-sump engine. The adoption of this lubrication system allowed the engine to sit lower still in the chassis; the addition of a twenty-liter oil tank (the previous wet sump held only seven liters) also provided better lubrication at a cooler temperature.

Other important innovations were hidden behind the engine. The presence of a five-speed gearbox was revealed in the cockpit by a superb chrome-plated gate with six notches. Two Watts linkages reinforced the rear axle and the tires were dramatic in size.

Was the latest berlinetta more of an improvement on the racing 250GT rather than a

The four-liter engine was tried out in the GTO and the 330LM but never managed to unseat the three-liter engine.

Out of a total of thirty-eight GTOs made, nine were sold in England, with right-hand drive, including 3969 GT, which began its career at the London Salon in 1962.

fully new car? It is true that the hundred vehicles required for homologation had been produced in 1960 and 1961. It is also true that some of the characteristics of this latest model were recorded on the 1961 homologation forms. The surprise—or the admiration—caused by this "omolagazione" 250GT took the form of an "O" which was added to the name of the car.

The craftsmen who produced this impressive transformation were absent from the ceremony. An obscure dispute a few days prior led to the departure of eight of the engineers, Bizzarrini at their head. On that day, the GTO also lacked the spoiler that was to surmount its truncated rear. It must have been thought that this aerodynamic device, which was improvised on many Ferraris in 1961—and on the Pininfarina berlinetta at the Le Mans practices—was out of place with the new body. At the first public appearance of the GTO at Sebring on March 24, 1962, however, a tail spoiler was solidly riveted to the beautiful body.

This first appearance of the GTO, one month to the day after its presentation, ended in an incontestable success. Olivier Gendebien and Phil Hill, Ferrari's magical team in endurance races, finished in second place in the wake of a Testa Rossa driven by Joakim Bonnier and Lucien Bianchi. For the record, this 1961 Testa Rossa belonged to Count Volpi, whose Scuderia Serenissima had taken on the eight Maranello renegades. Giotto Bizzarrini was thus present, as a rival, at the success of his creation.

Even if Hill and Gendebien had not gone full bore with the GTO in this twelve-hour race, no one underestimated its potential. The power of this Maranello stallion was only ever increased by about ten horsepower more than the best berlinettas from 1961, but it immediately proved to be faster, more reliable and more maneuverable.

At the Targa Florio, the second round of the world championship, the Gran Turismo category (and the overall fourth place) fell to GTO 3451 GT belonging to a lawyer from Trieste, Italy, Pietro Ferraro. This was the first appearance and the first win by a private GTO.

Ferrari now left the field open to its customers and the factory no longer took part in the Gran Turismo championship—except on rare occasions, generally to test an experimental car. This occurred most notably with the two four-liter GTOs at the Nurburgring 1,000 Kilometer race and the Le Mans twenty-four-hour race, but had no influence at all on the result of the world championship. The most formidable opponents of the GTOs remained the GTOs.

You only live twice

—

It was the failure of the 250LM to achieve Gran Turismo homologation that led to the development of the 250GTO 64.

On December 1, 1962, Enzo Ferrari announced that he intended to halt production of the GTO in 1963; he judged it to be too fast for the great majority of drivers. It is true that he was preparing several replacements for the supreme GT, including the powerful 330LM with its four-liter engine. Nevertheless, 1963 saw ten other GTOs leave Maranello to add to the twenty-five built in 1962. The list of successes continued to grow as well, despite the efforts of Aston Martin, Jaguar and AC Cobra, and despite the ephemeral 330LM.

The private GTOs brought a second world title to Ferrari in 1963, but the horizon of 1964 looked dark. With chassis that were often just as good and engines that were of greater capacity and often more powerful, the Astons, Jaguars and Cobras with American engines began to threaten. Ferrari's response came at the Paris Salon in October 1963; the 250LM caught everyone unaware. A 250GT with a mid-engine, directly derived from the proto-

types that had dominated their class that season, would be a terror among the old front-engine GTs. Yet before descending onto the racetrack, the 1964 championship was played out around the conference table; the Commission Sportive Internationale (CSI) refused pointblank to homologate the 250LM.

Condemned to compete against prototypes, the LM suddenly lost its raison d'etre—with the result that the GTO regained its own.

The 250GTO 64 shared common elements with the 250LM, which it was to replace at a moment's notice. Its body bore no signature, but Pininfarina, who had signed the mid-engine GT body, could not disown it and the GTO 64 was not lacking in elegance.

The development of the new GTO was entrusted to engineer Mauro Forghieri. While the new car's exterior may have been unrecognizable, the chassis and mechanics remained frozen in their 1962 state due to the regulations. The CSI in fact only authorized the widening of

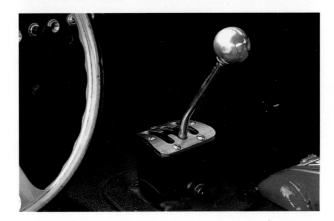

the wheel track, made necessary by the use of wider rims and tires—from 15×6 at the front and 15×6.5 at the rear to 15×6.5 and 15×7.5, respectively. For the same reasons, the mechanicals were only subjected to minor adjustments.

Despite its different origin—stylistic and no longer only technical—the new body aimed at making the same advances as the 1962 had; improving still further the aerodynamics while reducing weight. As far as the latter was concerned, the body was slightly lowered and widened a fraction but above all, shortened by 190 mm. On the other hand, the shorter, less-plunging nose and the return to a wide radiator grille seemed to have a negative effect, despite the windshield inclining as far back as possible.

Only three 250GTO 64s were produced, the three last GTOs. They were built simultaneously and numbered 5571 GT, 5573 GT and 5675 GT. The first—the one pictured here—differed from the two others by having a lip on its roof, like the 250LM presented at the Paris Salon. As it was quite easy to "rejuvenate" the bodywork of the 1962 and 1963 GTOs, this

The interior appears familiar, but the airfoil integrated into the roof is a peculiarity of 5571 GT, the first of the three GTO 64s.

The GTO, rejuvenated by driving

treatment was later applied to four of the earlier cars at Scaglietti's workshop, with an airfoil added to two of the GTOs and a longer roof to the other two.

Car 5571 GT, the first 250GTO 64, was thus ready at Daytona on February 12, for the opening of the 1964 championship. Entered by Scuderia Ferrari for Luigi Chinetti's North American Racing Team (NART) and driven by Phil Hill and Ricardo Rodriguez, it won an outright victory, far ahead of Carroll Shelby's Cobras. At Sebring, six weeks later, Ferrari entered (under the colors of Scuderia Centro-Sud, this time) the second GTO 64, 5573 GT, with Carlo Abate and Jean Guichet, but they were disqualified. With 5571 GT having become the property of Luigi Chinetti's NART, Richardo Rodriguez, David Piper and Gammino finished seventh, behind the prototype Ferraris, but also behind the Cobras. Never-

theless, they salvaged something from the wreckage by winning Class III of the world championship.

After its victory at Daytona and the disappointing result at Sebring, 5571 GT was only seen three other times. At Le Mans, Jose Rosinski lost the differential in a scatter over the track. Under the winter sun of Bermuda, Phil Hill landed tenth place in the Nassau Trophy and Pedro Rodriguez ended the racing career of 5571 GT with a sixth place in the Nassau Tourist Trophy.

In fact, the Sebring result anticipated the final classification of the 1964 championship: the GTO had to make do with Class III, reserved for GTs of less than three liters. Its qualities, however great they were, were not enough to make up for the difference in capacity with the large American engines. Enzo Ferrari was conscious of this and after having committed himself in the last season more than he ever had before, he abandoned the 250GTO to its two and a half titles and, through the 250GTO 64, also GT racing.

Thus, the 250LM having bungled its entrance, the GTO remains the last Gran Turismo Ferrari specially designed for racing.

Two years ago, the first of the 250GTO 64s came to join 3869 GT at Albert Obrist's home.

At Daytona, Phil Hill and Ricardo Rodriguez drive 5571 GT to outright victory.

Modest perfection

The third generation of Ferrari mid-engine prototypes managed to contain the arrival of Ford.

Its finish is as well turned out as its profile. Impeccable red paint, a beautifully curved glass windshield, seats upholstered with bright blue cloth—an attention to detail carried as far as the polished aluminum trim surrounding the body. It seems that the 1964 Ferrari prototypes were so perfect that the men at Maranello even had time to see to the smallest details. The Fords were only just arriving.

The 275/330Ps made for the 1964 season were more than ever a development of the 250Ps which, during the previous season, had brought Ferrari its eighth world title. With this success behind them, there was no need for a completely new design. This explains the modest perfection of the 1964 Ps.

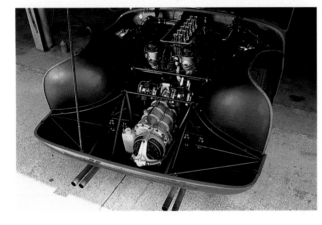

In three seasons, the Ferrari concept of the mid-engine reached maturity and 1964 was a year of consolidation.

The tubular chassis of these prototypes is an inheritance from the first Ferrari with a central engine, the 1960 Dino 246F1. In three years it evolved progressively, using various V-6 engines, some V-8s and finally the 1963 V-12. The traditional ladder side frames thus gave way to a cradle of triangulated tubes, made rigid in several places by riveted aluminum panels. The two fuel tanks which were lodged under the door sills of the 250P were moved back to either side of the engine to provide optimum balance, while the radiators at the front counterbalanced the weight on the rear axle-tree. A surprising detail, but one that obviously responded to economy of weight, was the use of some chassis tubes as pipes for the circulation of water and oil between the radiators and the mechanical compartment. The wheelbase returned to the fateful 2400 mm. There were four wide Borrani spoked wheels with Dunlop disc brakes, inboard at the rear, and suspended independently by means of wishbones and the combination of tubular, adjustable shock absorbers with coil over shock suspension.

The V-12 engine was placed lengthwise in the rear understructure. The five-speed axle-mounted gearbox, contained in the same cas-

Less weight, more power

ing as the self-locking differential, neighbored it. The clutch went at the very back.

The three new chassis made for 1964—0818, 0820 and 0822—were not so different from those of the 250Ps of 1963. Indeed, so similar were they, that three of the latter—0812, 0814 and 0816—were re-used by the Ferrari team itself. On the other hand, their bodies made it easy to distinguish among them, the 1964 ones having windshields with uprights inclined toward the back, airfoil targa-type bars of a simpler design and a rear hood that tipped forward rather than backward.

▎ Two V-12s for the same car

It was the engine more than the chassis that constituted the innovation of the 1964 vintage. The three-liter engine of the 250P, more similar to that of the GTO, was abandoned and two other V-12s replaced it: a 3.3 liter and a four-liter. The 3.3 liter engine was obtained by a new bore that brought the capacity to 3285 cc, some 275 cc per cylinder. With a compression ratio of 9.8:1, it had 320 horsepower at 7700 rpm. The four-liter engine, which had already been experimented with on various occasions, returned to the 77 mm bore with a 71 mm stroke, taking its capacity to 3967 cc, 330 cc per cylinder. But with six 42 mm instead of 38 mm carburetors and a compression ratio reduced to 9:1, it was credited with 390 horsepower at 7500 rpm. Another important difference was the weight. The 275P registered 1,665 lb. dry compared with 1,730 lb. for the 330P.

The cylinder capacities once more gave these cars their name, but not without imprecision. On the one hand, the chassis were not

differentiated as to either 1963 or 1964 vintage. On the other hand, the engines were interchangeable. Therefore, the vintage of the chassis is added to the car's name.

In 1964, Ferrari only entered three of the four races for the Prototype world championship, but won all three of them. At Sebring, Michael Parkes and Maglioli brought in a 275P 63 in front of an identical car driven by Ludovico Scarfiotti and Nino Vaccarella. John Surtees and Lorenzo Bandini's 330P 64 took third place.

At the Nurburgring 1,000 Kilometer race, the three cars entered were of the 1964 type, all in the 3.3 liter version. Scarfiotti and Vaccarella were the winners in 0820. Finally, at Le Mans, the 3.3 liter engine once more stood out, but this time on a 1963 chassis, driven by Jean Guichet and Vaccarella, coming in before the 330P 64s driven by Hill/Bonnier and Surtees/Bandini.

After this brief but decisive championship, which earned Ferrari a ninth world title, all the Ps were sold to private stables; Maranello was to completely renew its arsenal for the 1965 season. Photographed here is 0820, Scarfiotti and Vaccarella's victorious mount at the Nurburgring. When it was sold to Luigi Chinetti's NART, it had swapped its 3.3 liter engine for a four-liter and had been painted in the American colors. Albert Obrist has returned it to its original "rosso corsa."

Scarfiotti and Vaccarella made an impression with 0820 at the Nurburgring despite a damaged airfoil.

Graham Hill and 0820 in American colors during the 1965 Sebring twelve-hour race.

A mile-eating beauty

A small P4 for racing customers.

The Dino 206S was presented at the same time as the 330P3, on the occasion of a press conference organized at Maranello in February 1966. Sporting regulations at that time provided for two categories within the world championship: the world prototype Group 6 challenge and the Group 4 international championship of Sports racing car makers. In Group 6, no consideration of homologation quantity came into play; in Group 4, a minimum of fifty cars had to have been made. The suffix "S" which Ferrari added to the Dino 206 was thus explicit: a production of fifty of these Sports racing cars was envisaged and this obviously implied that they would have to be marketed. Nothing happened as planned.

Enzo Ferrari perpetuated the memory of his son after his death in 1956, by giving the diminutive form of his name to a 1500 cc engine with six cylinders in a sixty-five-degree Vee. The Dino badge, however, only appeared in place of the Cavallino in 1965, on the front of the 166S, which soon became the 206SP, and

whose engine was only a descendant of that first V-6 conceived at Maranello. In its original configuration, the Dino 206S was directly derived from the 206SP with which Scarfiotti had taken the 1965 mountain championship of Europe from Porsche. Equipped with new cylinder heads with hemispherical combustion chambers, the 1987 cc V-6 with its four overhead camshafts abandoned dual ignition, and indirect Lucas injection gave way to three triple Weber 40D CN2 carburetors. The compression ratio fell from 12.5:1 to 10.8:1 without effecting the horsepower, which remained near 220 at 9000 rpm.

The chassis, like that of the P3, was in the form of a structure of triangulated tubes strengthened by riveted aluminum panels, with some plastic panels around the cockpit. The aluminum body was made by Piero Drogo's Carrozzeria Sports Car at Modena, like that of the P3, to which it is similar, both in design and conception. Compared to the 206SP, the 206S retained the 2290 mm wheelbase but, with the larger wheel tracks, it was

wider, longer and higher. The 1,279 lb. weight remained favorable.

It was not the imposing P3, a prototype whose use was reserved exclusively for the factory, which offended the agile Dino, but the fact that it could not be homologated to Group 4. Like the prototypes, it was now excluded, and its production was limited. Ferrari managed nevertheless to sell sixteen or seventeen 206Ss in a separate batch, beginning with chassis number 002 and finishing with 032 or

034. This total includes the three or four which were kept and raced by the factory. These cars are the most interesting ones, because their continuous evolution reflected the potential of this little Ferrari. Car 004, owned by Dudley Mason-Styrron, is photographed here; it is one of the factory cars and its story is fascinating.

The first known appearance of 004 dates back to the 1966 Targa Florio when it was equipped with an injected engine and dual ignition. Driven by Parkes and Scarfiotti, it

Car 004, the second of this type made, was used by the factory team in 1966 and 1967.

166

Car 004 at the Targa Florio and at the Nurburgring 1,000 Kilometer race in 1966.

failed when in third place due to a leak in its fuel tank. One month later, repaired but with the same technical configuration, it raced at the Nurburgring. At its wheel, Scarfiotti and Bandini surprised everyone by coming in second behind Phil Hill's Chaparral. At the 1,000 Kilometers of Monza in 1967, 004 was entrusted to two new hopes, Gunther Klass and Jonathan Williams, and had an engine with three valves per cylinder and a modified injection system. The engine failed, however, when Klass was leading the two-liter class.

At the Nurburgring 1,000 Kilometer race, one month later, 004 was assigned to the Scarfiotti/Klass team. It was equipped for the occasion with a 2.4 liter engine with three valves and injection borrowed from the Formula 1 car with which Scarfiotti had entered the German Grand Prix in that very same place the year before. With this engine, which could attain 275 horsepower at 8000 rpm, the little Ferrari reached the height of its development and a terrain more appropriate to its

▮ It carried the Ferrari insignia

agile strength than the German circuit could not be imagined. It no longer bore the Dino badge at the front, but the Ferrari insignia— no more, no less. Unfortunately, a piston broke during practice and it was not possible to repair 004 before the race.

Whether intentionally or not, the reappearance of the Ferrari insignia put an end to the Dino experiment in racing.

The ideal berlinetta

▬

At the 1964 Paris Salon, the arena was set for Ferrari. In Formula 1, at the end of the Mexican Grand Prix, John Surtees had been hailed as the world champion with the 158F1. In the Sports racing class, Graham Hill and Joakim Bonnier had just won the Paris 1,000 Kilometers with a 330P. Finally, in the Gran Turismo category, another Ferrari, the GTO driven by Berger and Bianchi, won the Tour de France for the tenth time in the ninth consecutive year.

With its truncated rear, streamlined headlights, sleek windshield, bucket seats, gear lever and hungry-looking grille, the new berlinetta—which was attracting all the attention on the Ferrari stand—did not conceal its pretensions. The car was clearly more inclined toward racing than the 1963 250GT Lusso it was succeeding. Nor did the 275GTB try to hide its sporting heredity. This characteristic was manifested as much by its power unit as by its transmission and suspension.

The most important innovation was the 3.3 liter V-12 engine, which succeeded the great three-liter 250GT. The latest stage in the evolution of the V-12 that was created in 1947, this 3285.7 cc engine was derived from the one that had made the prototype 275Ps of the past season practically invincible. The increased capacity resulted from changing the bore from 73 to 77 mm, while the stroke remained at 58.8 mm.

The differences between the 3.3 liter racing engines and that of the new berlinetta, Tipo 213, are numerous. The road car was without the classic dry sump, sported a 9.2:1 compression ratio, and three Weber 40 carburetors, type 40 DCZ/6 or 40 FI/1. Its 280 horsepower compared with more than 310 for the 275P. This nevertheless represented an increase of nearly twenty horsepower compared with the 250GT Lusso. In any case, for skeptics, there also existed an option with six 40 DCN3 Weber carburetors, promising an extra ten horsepower.

The chassis, designated Tipo 563, is typical of Ferrari with its ladder of oval tubes doubled by the superstructure of triangulated cross

A feline profile inherited from the 250GTO.

The six twin-choke carburetors and Borrani wire spoke wheels were optional. The short nose was, on the other hand, a characteristic of the GTBs of 1964 and 1965.

braces. Yet independent rear suspension was novel, making its first appearance on a road Ferrari. The rigid rear axle setup thus gave way to wishbones whose movement was controlled by a telescopic shock absorber and helical spring combination acting on the upper wishbone.

To provide a better distribution of weight between the front and the rear, the gearbox was no longer coupled to the engine, but to the differential and combined in one casing. This was a practice that Ferrari had adapted to its single-seaters at the beginning of the fifties and to some Sports racing cars a little later. Moreover, the box had five synchronized gears; until then, the five gears had only been obtained—on road Ferraris—by means of an overdrive on the fourth. Control was provided by a stick placed to the left of the transmission tunnel and the selection—second is opposite third and fourth is opposite fifth—is guided by a gate, as with the GTO.

People who mourned the loss of the great Borrani wheels with their chrome-plated spokes and polished aluminum rims could now rejoice in the more resistant, light alloy Campagnolo wheels, which diminished the non-suspended weight and made maintenance easier. Wire wheels were still available, however, as an option, reference RW 3874.

The euphoria of the sixties

Pininfarina's classic design, shaped by Scaglietti, provoked some criticism, but these seem to have been calmed with the passage of time. Twenty years later, Pininfarina's GTB has become a sort of ideal berlinetta, an example of elegance without aggressiveness.

Euphoria dominated the Ferrari stand at the 1964 Paris Salon. Despite its stiff price tag the Ferrari 275GTB appeared to a receptive world. It was also a changing world. After ten years, the Mercedes 300SL (3,258 of them were made) had been withdrawn. Jaguar had increased the engine capacity of its E-type from 3.8 to 4.2 liters; Aston Martin increased that of its DB5 to five liters; and Maserati revealed a cabriolet version of its Mistral as if to echo the 275GTS that Ferrari presented at the same time as the GTB. Finally, a new Italian manufacturer, Lamborghini, appeared on the scene with the 350 GT.

At Maranello, orders were not slow to flood in, and it took nearly three months to satisfy

The 275GTB was the first road Ferrari with independent rear suspension.

them. The first GTB delivered to France (chassis number 6457) arrived in January 1965. It was dark green—red was much less popular than it is today.

The production of the 275GTB reached 250 vehicles before the first significant alterations were made. The first of these concerned the transmission shaft which, between the clutch and the axle-mounted gearbox, acquired a Cardan joint at each end. The rigid mounting had caused difficulties: if the alignment of the engine and the gearbox—obtained by using shims to adjust the attachment of the engine to the chassis—was not perfect, harmful vibrations would result. The substitution of a shaft with Hooke's joints simplified these adjustments, but it was only a temporary solution.

Although apparently an aesthetic change, the remodeled front had in fact a more significant intention in counteracting the tendency

The gear lever is guided by a gate, as in the GTO, but the gearbox is in unit with the differential.

of the nose to lift at speed. Scaglietti's definitive version appeared at the 1965 Paris Salon with an elongated nose reducing the radiator grille to an ellipse and making new fenders necessary. Other changes included more generous dimensions for the rear window and new hinges on the trunk to replace the cumbersome earlier ones. The adjustments made to the trunk were also combined with a new fuel tank in two parts, which were lodged in the fenders and between which the spare wheel was placed horizontally.

There were also some changes in details. Included were a larger flywheel, a new self-locking ZF differential, a Borg & Beck diaphragm clutch instead of the Fichtel & Sachs one, new fastenings for the shock absorbers and springs, and new valve guides in the cylinder heads to reduce the typical Ferrari smoke.

In the cockpit, a Nardi steering wheel with guilloche arms replaced the one with open-work arms. All-leather seats became standard once more, imitation leather and cloth seats only being available as an option. Later, it was the wheels that changed; the Campagnolos with radial gills gave way to other Campagnolos of simpler design and maintenance.

■ Evolution without revolution

In the spring of 1966, the 275GTB underwent an important modification: the transmission shaft was enclosed in a torque tube which combined the engine and the axle-mounted gearbox into one rigid unit which was fixed to the chassis at four points, two for the gearbox and two for the engine (instead of four before). These new fixing points required a new engine block and a new gearbox casing. As for the chassis, it had to be redesigned to accommodate them.

Thus, even if the appearances had changed little, the 275GTB Series II was a new car. Nevertheless, no more than 100 Series II cars were made; the prototype of the 275GTB/4 had already made an appearance at Maranello. Production of the 275GTB ended in June 1966.

Significant advances are concealed beneath a longer hood.

The engine is still in front

It was not Scaglietti's handiwork that marked the new 3.3 liter Ferrari berlinetta from the previous one on the stand at the 1966 Paris Salon. On the contrary, the main innovation was well concealed beneath an imperceptible bulge in the hood. It was the adoption of a valve system with four overhead camshafts that brought about the 275GTB/4, progress that was inversely proportional to appearances.

Only the block—fixed at two points—of the last GTB was retained; the cylinder heads and almost everything else were totally new. In the cylinder heads, the camshafts now drove the tappets directly, following the method tested on the 3.3 liter and four-liter engines of the P2 prototypes in the 1965 season. Their chain drive required a different engine front cover. For the fuel supply, the six Weber 40 DCN carburetors were mounted on lengthened manifolds. Finally, the dry-sump lubrication system, tested on the racing 275GTBs, made a reappearance in this engine, Tipo 226. A tank connected to a special radiator increased the quantity of lubricant in circulation from ten to more than sixteen liters, providing better cooling and thus more efficient lubrication. This tank, normally lodged in the front right fender,

was accessible through the hood. On the right-hand-drive version, such as the car shown here, the position of the tank changed sides.

As for the rest, there was little change. But had not the main evolutionary work been done on the previous version of the GTB, hardly a year before? The GTB/4 thus retained the Tipo 596 chassis to which the engine and axle-mounted gearbox were fixed at four points.

Details such as the replacement of the wood on the dashboard by leather and the option of electric windows could be mentioned, but the main progress was obviously in the potential of this new road berlinetta, the first production Ferrari to be sold with four camshafts. It was claimed to have 300 horsepower at 8000 rpm, but this figure—which, in any case, was fairly optimistic—was much less significant than the considerable improvement in torque, maneuverability and steering.

Would this be enough in the face of the daring Miura that Lamborghini had announced at the Geneva Salon six months before? The new arrival's Miura was indeed a revolution. The car also had a V-12 engine, also with four camshafts, but in a transverse, mid-position. The body was extremely low, designed by Marcello

Four overhead camshafts for higher performance and increased tractability.

Gandini for Bertone, and the colors were brilliant—yellow, orange and apple green. Was this provocation? Ferrari and Pininfarina made their response with the later 365, but in its absence, it fell to the 275GTB/4 alone to take up the challenge. How did it fare in this attempt?

As far as the stopwatch was concerned, the four-liter Lamborghini dominated the 3.3 liter Ferrari, particularly as regards the maximum speed, 250 km/h compared with 270. But the Ferrari was unanimously considered to be less "critical" for driving and infinitely more civilized than its modernistic rival. The sales figures were also to the Ferrari's advantage, but only over a brief period of common existence: in 1967, over 250 GTB/4s were sold compared with 110 Miuras. The short career of the four-cam Ferrari berlinetta—350 cars produced between the autumn of 1966 and the spring of 1968—distorts the comparison somewhat. American standards, which were increasingly severe and irreconcilable with the "small" 3.3 liter engine, certainly played a role in the premature eclipse of the 275, but so did the Miura. The 365GTB/4 Daytona would later take up the baton and, with its engine still in front but increased from 3.3 to four liters, it would solve two problems at once: more power and consequently greater adaptability to American specifications.

Open to the air

Opening the 275GTB/4 to the air—an idea of Luigi Chinetti's, the US importer and creator of NART.

From the time of its launch in October 1964, the 275GTB, a true berlinetta with its cockpit snugly enclosed, was combined with an elegant, sophisticated convertible alternative, the 275GTS. Although also designed by Pininfarina, but created at Turin and not at Scaglietti's workshop, the convertible body in fact had no connection with that of the berlinetta. Moreover, its 3.3 liter V-12 engine lost about twenty horsepower. A lower rear axle ratio partially compensated for this loss, but not as far as the top speed was concerned. In all respects, the 275GTS was therefore clearly less of a sports car than the 275GTB. Its name, GTS (S for spyder), was also somewhat misleading. As regards a spyder, it was a real cabriolet, with wind-up side windows, deflectors, proper heating and a luxury top. The gap widened in October 1966, when the 275GTB was replaced by the 275GTB/4 and the 275GTS by the 330GTS. Heavier than the four-cam 275, the four-liter V-12 made the 330GTS more supple, refined and urbane.

It was in this context that Luigi Chinetti intervened. Chinetti was a pioneer, victorious racer, indestructible sportsman, dynamic organizer and the Ferrari importer for the United States, which had long been Ferrari's main market. Chinetti had an idea paralleling his plan of 1958 which had led to the Spyder California. He would construct a convertible version of the current berlinetta. He thus first obtained a 275GTB/4 from Scaglietti. The operation was carried out with the utmost simplicity, as regards both the mechanics and the structure; nothing was changed apart from some body panels. These minimal changes were intended to remain faithful to the spirit of the berlinetta's designers. They worked well, and the original convertible retained all the charm of a berlinetta. The differences were subtle. The car was open to the air and it had the small enameled insignia of the North American Racing Team on the back.

The first 275GTB/4 NART Spyder arrived in New York in February 1967, and Chinetti could not resist the temptation of entering the beautiful cabriolet in the Sebring twelve-hour race. Scuderia Ferrari, which had triumphed

at Daytona a few weeks earlier, had abandoned this second round of the world championship in Florida. In a field of few Ferraris, the performance of the NART stood out all the more. Driven by journalist Denise McCluggage and "Pinky" Rollo, it came in seventeenth and was the only Ferrari at the finish—an honorable performance on the part of such a civilized car.

A few months later, *Road & Track* published an account of a test drive of this same car under the laudatory title of "Ferrari 275GTS/4 NART, the most satisfying sports car in the world." Compared with the 275GTS, which had been test driven a year before, performance had improved in all areas and the maximum speed had increased from 233 to 249 km/h. The magazine also announced that the production was limited to twenty-five vehicles, available exclusively via Chinetti.

The 275GTB/4 NART—275GTB/4S NART or NART Spyder, depending on the source—did not in fact ever appear in any Ferrari publications. The imprecise designation of this non-standard Ferrari is perhaps caused by this omission, and the refusal of official recognition by Ferrari is not unrelated to the limited circulation of this car; we know today that

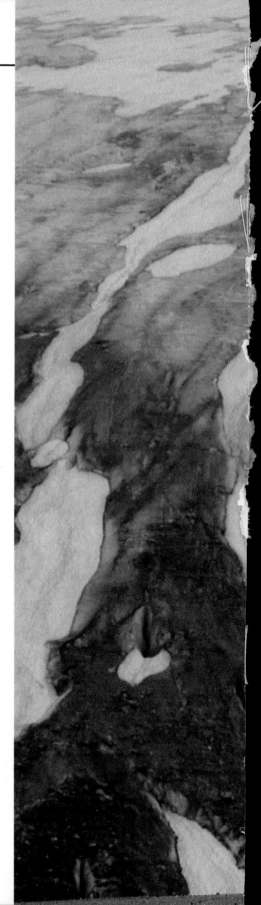

Here is a list of the ten true NART Spyders.

Prototype car 09437 was sold in North Carolina, after Sebring and the *Road & Track* road test. It remains there with its first owner.

Car 09751 was sold in Connecticut. It is today in New Jersey with its third owner.

Car 10139 was sold in Florida, where it is to be found with its fourth owner.

Car 10219 was sold in Illinois. It has never changed hands.

Car 10249 was sold in Illinois. It remains there with an owner who may be the first.

Car 10453 was sold to Steve McQueen. The car is still in California, with a second owner.

Car 10691 was sold in New York. It has never changed hands.

Car 10709 was sold in North Carolina. It is still with the same owner.

Car 10749 was sold in New York and resold in California ten years later.

Car 11057, the tenth and last specimen, is the car pictured here. This car is the only one not to be sold in the United States, the only one not in the United States today, and Albert Obrist's only Ferrari that is not red.

Ferrari or not, the way this superb and very rare creature has won the devotion of its fans has to be acknowledged.

only ten of them were made. This low number cannot be explained any other way, if we compare it to the numbers of the official spyder which succeeded it and easily passed the 250 mark. This is also reflected today in the way some people secretly try to "open up" innocent GTBs.

Ferrari's response to the Miura from Lamborghini was not so long in coming as a real equivalent to it was. At the 1966 Paris Salon where the 275GTB/4 appeared, Pininfarina exhibited on its own stand an important berlinetta with a mid-engine. Yet the highlight of this strange white creation was the cockpit. The large surface area of glass, increased by the transparent roof, served only to highlight the attraction of having three front seats—the driver's being exactly in the middle, with a passenger seat on either side!

Lamborghini was advocating the central engine; Ferrari and Pininfarina replied with the "central everything." The concept worked for the engine—a V-12 of course, longitudinal and not transverse—but why not the driver's seating as well? And why not three seats for the price of two? The caricaturist Russell Brockbank immediately published a cartoon showing a handsome Italian flanked by two attractive women who looked distinctly annoyed.

With this trick, Ferrari showed that it was quite familiar with mid-engines but that, as far as road GTs were concerned, front engines seemed preferable—for the time being.

In the meantime, the 365P Guida Centrale had been made. In fact, its development cannot have caused too many problems at Mara-

Three-seater

nello, where the racing department had a vast reserve of designs at its disposal. The chassis shared the same characteristics as the 250LM, including the fuel tank. The dimensions were increased, however, resulting in a wheelbase of 2600 mm instead of 2400. The steering wheel was placed in the middle with the help of two additional universal joints.

Alongside the four liters of the Miura, a smaller capacity engine would have seemed mean. This was no trouble. The 4.4 liter engine, which had just been created for the large 365 California cabriolet and would later be used in the 365GT 2+2, would do the trick, even with only two camshafts and about 320 horsepower. Ferrari did not go so far as to make a

It could have been the first road Ferrari to be mid-engined, but it was not put into production.

Three front seats with the steering wheel in the middle. Only two cars were made, but this design by Pininfarina was repeated on a Dino 206GT, which was the first mid-engine GT to be produced at Maranello.

specific gearbox for this special car; a five-speed ZF was coupled to the large V-12, as in the 330P3 prototypes used that racing season which had just finished.

It is improbable that production of this model was ever planned, although this could easily have been possible, so little did it disturb the career of the front-engine berlinettas. We know today that the 275GTB/4 and, later, the 365GTB/4 did not suffer from it.

The star of the 1966 Paris Salon did not, however, limit itself to its role of Muira-beater. At the Turin Salon two months later, it was followed by the Dino Berlinetta GT. With a similar design and the same structure, this study with its V-6 mid-engine, which was provisionally longitudinal, and its normal two seats, was nothing other than the first prototype of the Dino 206GT. In 1967, this Dino became the first Ferrari road berlinetta with a central engine—although a twelve-cylinder, mid-engined Ferrari was not marketed until 1971.

In the meantime, two copies of the three-seater berlinetta, which was also called Tris Speciale, were made in response to an order from Gianni Agnelli, chairman of Fiat. For one reason or another, the industrialist only took delivery of the first, 8815, in August. The

Impressive width, enough for three people abreast—almost.

Mid-engine, a pointer to the future

second, 8971, was finished at the end of September, just in time to be sent to Paris.

After the great interest the 365P Guida Centrale caused at the Paris Salon, it was sold in the United States by Luigi Chinetti, who did not miss the opportunity of buying it back some ten years ago and now keeps it in his exceptional collection of rare cars. Luigi Chinetti, Jr., has recently restored it to its original white color, and he was behind the wheel when it was photographed.

The first car, which was metallic gray, was equipped with a large spoiler spanning the entire width of the rear, on the orders of its illustrious owner, who considered the rear of the vehicle to be unstable. It was resold by the factory to an American in about 1970 and is still in the United States today.

The fact that two people closely linked to Ferrari had an interest in it lends still more importance to this berlinetta which was central to the story of road Ferraris—it marked the end of the front-engined berlinettas and the start of the era of mid-engines.

Space ship

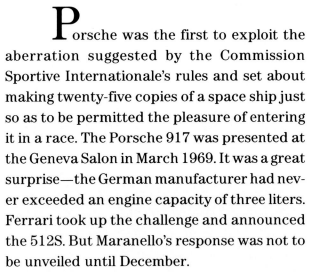

Porsche was the first to exploit the aberration suggested by the Commission Sportive Internationale's rules and set about making twenty-five copies of a space ship just so as to be permitted the pleasure of entering it in a race. The Porsche 917 was presented at the Geneva Salon in March 1969. It was a great surprise—the German manufacturer had never exceeded an engine capacity of three liters. Ferrari took up the challenge and announced the 512S. But Maranello's response was not to be unveiled until December.

When the fifty-first Italian salon opened its doors in Turin on October 29, 1969, the Porsche 917 was already well known. Not only had it been seen at Geneva eight months earlier, but it had even entered its first races, whereas Ferrari's project remained a mystery. Thus the yellow machine that Pininfarina presented on its stand at Turin caused a stir.

Designated the 512S, the descriptive leaflet revealed characteristics that were identical to those announced for the twenty-five five-liter Sports cars: forty-eight valves, a 4993 cc engine, 11:1 compression ratio, indirect Lucas fuel injection and 550 horsepower at 8000 rpm. It could also be guessed from the position of the seats—which were close to the centerline of the car and the large doors concealing fuel tanks—that this was indeed a racing chassis. The 2400 mm wheelbase and tracks also fit the Sports racing car bill.

How had Pininfarina managed to obtain a chassis at such a late hour? For what purpose was this strange machine—less than one meter high—made? Certainly the marketing of twenty-five monsters that could only be used for racing was preposterous, even though the price that was to be announced, $55,000, seems like a bargain today. Would a road version have enlarged the target and thus helped to market it? Such a road version would need

■ Aerodynamics is everything

Like the engine, the cockpit had its own hood, which opened in the opposite direction.

numerous alterations. The instruction manual for the 512S was eloquent. Under the heading "cold starting," for example, it was recommended to have a back-up battery, a hair dryer to heat up the injection distributor, a "start pilot" spray and another vehicle to tow the car in fifth so as to make the oil circulate before attempting to start the engine. An uninformed man was a man without a 512.

None of this applied to this 512S Berlinetta Speciale when it arrived on the salon stages. This was to be the road version of the 512S, but the engine was empty and the car was not for sale. This was merely a study in design made in collaboration with the Polytechnic Center of Turin, at a time when Pininfarina did not yet have an integrated wind tunnel. In fact, the front and the side sections of this superb shape differed little from one another and represented an excellent aerodynamic profile. It was soon discovered that this was not the case for the racing model of the 512, at least in the beginning.

It is surprising that Pininfarina never considered this avant-garde car important enough to keep its wonderful shape in the carrozzeria's collection. Today it is the pride of the Musee de l'Automobiliste, at Mougins on the French Riviera.

Holiday work

In April 1969, engineer Mauro Forghieri was on holiday when he received a telephone call from the Commendatore: "Mauro, we need a five-liter Sports racing car for the 1970 world championship. . . ." A new adventure was at hand.

Forghieri set to work, assembly work rather than pure design. And there was little time. The first round of the 1970 championship, the Daytona twenty-four-hour race, was to take place on January 31, allowing less than eight months to catch up with Porsche and, unlike Porsche, no chance of testing the new car in a race in 1969. But, also unlike its German rival, Maranello had more than one large-capacity car in its reserves. The 612 Can-Am, the Group 6 car made in 1968 to take part in the series of North American races, was used to provide most of the constituent elements of the five-liter Sports racing car. Starting with the V-12 engine with four camshafts, forty-eight valves and Lucas injection, the capacity was reduced from 6222 cc to 4993. The horsepower went from 620 to 550 at 8000 rpm.

The chassis also repeated the structure of the 612 with a central web of tubes and riveted aluminum sheets. The back was reduced to a classic understructure of tubes in which the engine, fixed at several points, added to the rigidity.

The season did not start off too badly. The 512 won at Sebring, but chronic aerodynamic woes, coupled with the often inadequate organization of the races, cut Ferrari's chances against Porsche.

Meanwhile, Forghieri continued to develop the 512, concentrating mainly on the aerodynamics and reducing weight. His modifications produced the 512M, which emerged successfully at the end of the season, boding well for 1971. But Ferrari centered the entire 1971 world championship on the development of a three-liter vehicle, the 312PB. The 512s were abandoned to private stables.

Some privateers put the 512M to good account. Kirk F. White organized a consortium of enthusiasts to buy 512S number 1040 (the 512s were numbered in a separate series from 1002 to 1050). White charged Penske Racing with preparing and entering it in the 1971 championship with Mark Donohue at the wheel. As meticulous as he was experienced,

The Sunoco 512, prepared by Roger Penske and driven by Mark Donohue, was the most serious rival to the Porsche 917s.

Roger Penske took the car totally apart and then rebuilt it up to his standards. He polished up every last detail of the Ferrari: suspension and steering ball joints, antiroll bar, electrical equipment; redesigned and cadmium-plated suspension arms; fitted dry-sump lubrication; and so on. Last but not least, the engine came back from Traco Engineering with about forty additional horsepower. A quick-fill gas system was also installed as were quick-release brakes, making brake pad changing fast at refueling stops. Compared to the $258,000 spent on this preparation, the $28,000 paid to the vendor looked like a tip.

The Sunoco blue Ferrari was enormously popular and was judged by many as the only serious rival to Porsche. With the impeccable Penske-White Ferrari, Donohue and David Hobbs were often faster than the best Porsche 917s and always the fastest among the Ferrari owners. But the team was plagued by bad luck. The blue 512 only competed in four races in the 1971 world championship: the Daytona twenty-four-hour race, the Sebring twelve-hour race, Le Mans and the Watkins Glen six-hour race. It started three times in pole position, but only finished twice; third at Daytona, after an accident which cost it one hour; and fourth at Sebring, after another collision.

Mauro Forghieri himself would have admitted that he had never seen such a well-prepared Ferrari.

The symmetries create interchangeable modules for the sake of both economy and purity of form.

"An automobile is first and foremost a dream"

W hen asked how he conceived of his automobiles, Enzo Ferrari once replied, "It is certain that the automobile was born from a dream—the dream that man once had for a different kind of mobility." Though this dream sometimes becomes dissipated and banal, a certain amount of fantasizing is involved in the conception of every automobile. In the study in architectural form that is the Modulo, Pininfarina expressed the eternal dream of a modular automobile, able to change function by substituting one or more modules, transforming itself into a sedan or a berlinetta, open or covered.

Designer Paolo Martin created the Modulo design and created a model in a 1:1 scale. When the modules are taken apart, the multiplicity of symmetries, both horizontal and vertical, is highlighted. The choice of the Ferrari 512S as the basis for this demonstration obviously gave the Modulo an even more daring image. With its wide wheels—incontestably derived from racing, but suggested rather than exposed—identical wheelbase and tracks, it gave the impression of power equivalent to that of the five-liter Sports racing car. An unworldly power.

To create the two successive 512s, Pininfarina used numerous pieces from Maranello, but only one single chassis tub, and he only used this as a model. The two studies by the Turin carrozzeria have bases of the same dimensions which are peculiar to them and onto which were grafted rolling axles and mechanical elements from the 512S, the engine and gearbox being empty. There being no further use for it, the precious chassis that had served as a model—probably number 1047—was handed over to Swiss driver Herbert Muller and was made into a real 512M.

The 512 had thus given its support to a non-competitive operation, displaying in a unique manner what racing can bring to the automobile.

Pininfarina has never parted with this Modulo, which in terms of design only had a limited influence on the carrozzeria's later creations. Judging by the effect it still has on the viewer, however, it may be that the future of the Modulo still lies before it.

Achevé d'imprimer
sur les presses de Graphing à Charleroi
en octobre 1988
Imprimé en Belgique